WORKING *the* PLATE

WORKING *the* PLATE

THE ART OF FOOD PRESENTATION

CHRISTOPHER STYLER

PHOTOGRAPHY BY DAVID LAZARUS

JOHN WILEY & SONS, INC.

Published by John Wiley & Sons, Inc., Hoboken, New Jersey
Published simultaneously in Canada

For general information about our other products and services, please contact our Customer Care Department within the United States at (800) 762-2974, outside the United States at (317) 572-3993 or fax (317) 572-4002.

Wiley also publishes its books in a variety of electronic formats. Some content that appears in print may not be available in electronic books. For more information about Wiley products, visit our web site at www.wiley.com.

Library of Congress Cataloging-in-Publication Data

Styler, Christopher
  Working the plate : the art of food presentation / Christopher Styler ;
photography by David Lazarus.
p. cm.
  Includes index.
  ISBN-13 978-0-471-47939-0 (cloth)
  ISBN-10 0-471-47939-X (cloth)
1.   Food presentation. 2.   Garnishes (Cookery) I. Title.
  TX652.S826 2006
  641.5—dc22

                                                                    2005015433

Printed in China

10 9 8 7 6 5 4 3 2 1

FOR OUR NEW NIECE LISA—
A LITTLE SLICE OF EVERYTHING
THAT'S RIGHT IN THE WORLD.

•

CONTENTS

INTRODUCTION
1

THE MINIMALIST
7

THE ARCHITECT
25

THE ARTIST
47

CONTEMPORY
EUROPEAN STYLE
65

ASIAN INFLUENCES
87

THE NATURALIST
105

DRAMATIC FLAIR
129

DESSERTS: CLASSIC
AND CONTEMPORARY
151

PAINTING THE PLATE:
SAUCES AND TECHNIQUES FOR FINISHING PLATES
185

INDEX
197

ACKNOWLEDGMENTS

I would like to thank the chefs who so generously shared their thoughts on the art of plating. As I hoped when I started this project, their insights, opinions, styles and preferences show the great range of possibilities in this particularly varied (and edible) art form. Contributing chefs' bios and views on working the plate are found dispersed throughout the chapters.

I had more fun working with David Lazarus in his studio than could be expected. Thanks to Dave and to Bruce Levin for introducing us.

Mariann Sauvion lent invaluable advice and skill to the plates you see in the dessert chapter.

Kim Yorio and Joseph Seoane did what they do best: make me happy and keep me in line.

Thank you to the people at Wiley (past and present) who made this happen: Susan Wyler, Justin Schwartz and Christine DiComo.

INTRODUCTION

t was over twenty years ago when I took my first non-restaurant job at a glossy national food magazine. The test kitchen lacked the excitement of a restaurant kitchen, but the knowledge I gained working with the most experienced cooks from around the world more than made up for that. There was one thing, though, I never adjusted to: the frequent trips to photo studios to shoot the finished versions of recipes I had developed or tested. Painting turkeys with soy sauce and then spraying them with hair-spray so the color would stay put until we "got the shot" was an alien concept. Working in restaurants, I had learned to make food beautiful in the seconds it took to get it from a hot sauté pan onto the guest's plate. Indeed, a restaurant chef's satisfaction comes immediately after preparing a dish, in that dramatic moment when an artfully arranged plate is set before a guest. *Working the Plate* is about that moment. It is not a book about food styling, but about the real-life art of *plating:* arranging harmonious components of a meal in a strikingly beautiful way.

There are as many approaches to the art of plating as there are talented chefs. *Working the Plate* takes a careful look at some of the main schools of thought in contemporary food presentation. Close-up color photographs show the finished presentation and, in each case, the steps taken to create these gorgeous plates.

Working the Plate is divided into sections, each devoted to a single style of plating. A word of warning: These categories were created in order to define broad styles of plating. I don't imagine any chef will agree with these categories completely and, more importantly, will identify wholly with one style or another. And that is one of the main points to remember as you look through this book. As the pictures that accompany each chapter illustrate, these styles are a way to think about the elements of a plate and how to present them. They are, in effect, a starting point for a dialogue on the art and principles of plating.

Food presentation goes beyond the arrangement of finished ingredients on a plate. In fact, you could argue that presentation is a direct outgrowth of a particular chef's style of cooking and the venue in which he or she practices that style. The chef in a casual neighborhood restaurant with a leaning toward the cooking of the Italian countryside is more likely to put together plates on which each ingredient is easily identifiable, with little embellishment, or in other words, in what I identify as the naturalist style. A chef running the kitchen of a four-star resort is likely to spend more time thinking about the preparation of plate elements and is more likely to lean toward dramatic presentations of one type or another. A chef's style is defined by (and evolves from) his or her work experience, personal aesthetics, and environment.

To reinforce this point, listen to the chefs featured throughout this book talk about their individual take on the art of plating. Yes, some identify closely with one style of plating or another, but many borrow from more than one school. (for that reason I did not try to assign a chef to a particular chapter; they are dispersed randomly through the book. One thing they all have in common is the realization that no one set of parameters can define any given chef's style, and that the art of plating is a personal one and one that is continually evolving.

Like the styles they illustrate, the photographs in this book are meant to be general guidelines pointing out the main features of a particular style. Take any finished plate from any chapter and use it to inspire your own creations: Accompanying each photograph is a brief overview of the presentation and the reasoning behind it. It is easy, using that reasoning, to create variations in arrangement, elements of the plate, and even the plate itself.

The recipes in the section that follow the section of photographs are also guidelines to creating the decorative elements of a plate. I've made use of these elements in the photographs throughout the book. Some, like the sauces and dressings, are used to "paint" or decorate the plates. Others, like the recipe for sautéed breast of chicken with warm salad (page 191; picture page 109), are a blueprint for a whole group of dishes prepared in the same style. Variations you can create are limited only by imagination and season.

Most of all, this book was intended as an introduction, and only an introduction, to various styles and schools of thought in the world of plated food. And with the creative arts of any kind, evolution is not only inevitable, but desirable. Explore.

MARCUS SAMUELSSON

Chef
Aquavit, Riingo
New York, NY

Thirty-three-year-old Marcus Samuelsson has received more accolades than most chefs receive in a lifetime: He was the youngest chef ever to receive a three-star restaurant review from *The New York Times,* in 1999 the James Beard Foundation honored him as best "Rising Star Chef," he was awarded a four-star rating in *Forbes* and a three-and-a-half-star rating in *Crain's,* and he was celebrated as one of "The Great Chefs of America" by The Culinary Institute of America. In 2001, Aquavit received a second three-star review from *The New York Times,* and in 2003 Samuelsson was awarded the James Beard Award for "Best Chef New York City."

And Samuelsson's cuisine continues to win national praise. He has been featured in *Gourmet, USA Today, Food & Wine, The New York Times, Australian Vogue Entertaining,* and *Bon Appetit,* and has appeared on CNN, The Discovery Channel, ABC's "Good Morning America," and several local New York television programs. He has written for *The New York Times'* "Chefs Column" and was also chosen to appear in an episode of The Culinary Institute of America's "Great Chefs" television series.

In addition to Aquavit, Marcus Samuelsson also focuses his energy on overseeing the AQ Cafe at Scandinavia House, and has recently opened Riingo, his new American-Japanese restaurant in the Alex Hotel on Manhattan's East Side. In the fall of 2003 Houghton Mifflin published his cookbook, *AQUAVIT and the New Scandinavian Cuisine.* On the philanthropic front, Samuelsson continues to act as the official spokesperson for the U.S. Fund for UNICEF in addition to working closely with C-CAP, where he is on the advisory board, as well as with the James Beard Foundation.

Photograph courtesy of Gediyon Kifle.

I think the plates we chefs create are essentially extensions of who we are. That's where we start when it comes to making creative decisions. Sweden and the rest of Scandinavia are more homogeneous, less diverse than many parts of the world. People tend to have similar views and opinions about a range of aspects of the culture, including art and design. This helped create a very strong aesthetic and sense of style that had a great effect on me when I was growing up in the '70s and '80s. Aesthetic is something that we Swedes think about a lot. I would define my style as minimalist, in terms of the visual sense, not in terms of portion.

My minimalist designs go with me no matter what the cuisine. I think aesthetics first. I think positive and negative space—how much of the plate will be covered, with, say, salad, and how much will be left open. Instead of "let's make this dish tall, or wide," I think about where your eye will fall when it hits the plate. To plate a gravlax dish, for example, I start with a white plate. If the dish is round, I'll cut the salmon square. So now you have a round white shape and a square pink shape. I'll dress the plate with black or purple mustard sauce, placed apart from the salmon so there is some space between them. That brings up a second point. Nothing is added or contrived in the plates. The purple mustard sauce, for example, is purple because we make it in-house and use red wine vinegar and purple mustard seed, not because I feel I need something purple on the plate.

I have a passion for art in general and find the art community inspiring. I think about plating like a painting: There should be something a little unexpected—such as the purple mustard sauce—along with the traditional ingredients. My cooking is a mix of traditional and contemporary techniques and styles, paired with the concept of the restaurant and my immediate environment. New York with all its museums, music scene, architecture, and creative energy overall is a great inspiration to me. The fusing of cultures, of styles of painting, of types of music is what interests me in life, in cooking, and in plating. I am inspired by flavors, art, and music from all over the world, but I am of course rooted in my experiences in Sweden and the US.

THE MINIMALIST

There is a scene in Kurt Vonnegut's novel *Breakfast of Champions* in which minimal painter Rabo Karabekian confronts a critic of his painting "The Temptation of Saint Anthony," a work in which a single stripe of colored tape runs vertically down a monotone canvas. Karabekian tells his critic, who had mentioned that his five-year-old could have produced it, that the band of color shows everything about a human being "which truly matters, with nothing left out."

The same can be said for minimalist plating. It is not necessarily about small portions, but about seeking to find the heart, the essence, of a dish.

Minimal design doesn't mean minimal flavor. Picture a cube of perfectly seared tuna set atop fresh corn relish and a pool of silky-smooth tomato coulis. A single bite delivers the crunch and sweetness of corn and red onion, the acidic note of tomato, and the warm richness of the fish. There is nothing minimal about that.

When pairing perfection with simplicity, little choices add up to a lot: Take the above plated tuna. The decision to create a plate with a cube-shaped rather than a more traditional rectangular cut of tuna may lead a chef to certain conclusions. If the plate is round, maybe a stripe of sauce rather than a circular pool will be more interesting. Setting the tuna on a little mound of salsa off to the side of the sauce will bring more visual excitement. If the plate is square, perhaps a round pool of sauce for contrast, and a smaller circle of salsa on which the tuna rests within the sauce is the answer. The decision of where to put the elements gains importance, too: Either of the above arrangements changes dramatically when placed dead center, slightly off-center, or along one edge of the plate.

Minimalist plating follows the growing trend among American chefs toward cleaner plates and simpler lines. Minimalism fits in nicely with another growing trend in restaurants: More (and smaller) courses, in the form of elaborate tasting menus, all "appetizer" menus, or dishes designed for sharing.

With the eye being drawn to a smallish (usually) construction set on a large (again, usually) plate, perfect ingredients are a must when it comes to plating in this style. That perfection can be innate—a plump oyster, flawlessly shucked and resting in its cupped shell—or created by the chef's skill—a single lamb chop, perfectly trimmed, seasoned, and seared to mahogany brown. There is a decided absence of finishing elements—sprigs of herbs, for example—for the sake of eye appeal. Visual drama is built into the food itself and the arrangement it is given on the plate.

The less there is on a plate, the more important each decision becomes, such as the size, shape, and color of the plate and the placement of the sauce/dressing, if any. These singular creations are usually set adrift on oversize plates—a further way to draw the eye to the main attraction and highlight the impact. When working with the ingredients or components of a plate, sometimes less is more.

PLATES PRESENTED

PAN-SEARED RED SNAPPER FILLET
with PARSLEY PESTO and RADISH SALAD

HERBED GOAT CHEESE with BLOOD
ORANGES and BALSAMIC REDUCTION

ROASTED ARTICHOKE BOTTOMS
with SHRIMP and HERBED MAYONNAISE

CHEF PROFILE: KENT RATHBUN

PAN-SEARED RED SNAPPER FILLET *with* PARSLEY PESTO *and* RADISH SALAD

Repetition is one way to stretch a minimalist idea into a larger serving size. Here, the austerity of simple geometric shapes—round pools of parsley pesto and triangles of red snapper—are given relief with a tangle of radish sprout and finely julienned radishes. Lining three of these small sculptures along a stretch of otherwise unadorned white plate enforces the minimalist aspects of the plate.

In this photograph, the three groupings are arranged in a straight line and off-center of a round plate, which adds two more geometric notes to the plate. Imagine the different impact of the same three groupings arranged lengthwise down the center of a rectangular plate. When plating, in the minimalist style or any other, shape and interest are contributed not only by the elements themselves, but by their arrangement on the plate and the shape of the plate itself.

Using a mandoline with the julienne blade in place, cut radishes into perfectly even, very thin matchsticks (about ⅛ x ⅛ x 2 inches); they should be roughly the length of the radish sprouts used for the salad. If you do not have a mandoline or a similar slicing tool, work carefully with a chef's knife, first slicing the radishes and then cutting them into strips as above.

Spoon three circles of parsley pesto onto the plate; leave space between the circles and place them down the center or off-center (as shown). Start with less pesto on the spoon than you think you need; it is always easier to add more pesto to a circle than to try to reduce the size of the circle.

Mound the radish salad toward one side of each circle of pesto; the salad should cover the edge of a pesto circle and a portion of the empty plate. Grasp the salad loosely with your fingertips to prevent crushing the vegetables and lower your hand almost to plate level before releasing the salad.

HERBED GOAT CHEESE
with BLOOD ORANGES *and* BALSAMIC REDUCTION

Minimalism has as much to do with the number of components on a plate as with how those components are treated. Here, four elements of a plate are assigned their own space, all related to one another but treated individually. Each element is framed on its own section of the plate: perfect drops of balsamic-honey glaze; an oval of chive-flecked goat cheese; lightly toasted French bread; and wedges of blood oranges in a vinaigrette made with their juice.

The idea behind this plate is essentially a deconstructed crostini. By separating the elements, we can look at each in its simplest form. In this particular plating, there is a nice play between the exactness of the goat cheese oval and precise drops, which are set at opposite compass points on the plate, and the free-form shapes of the stack of crostini and blood orange salad.

Using a paring knife, cut the segments from between the membranes of peeled blood oranges. Work over a bowl to collect the juices, which will be used to make the dressing (see page 186).

Using an oval scoop, set goat cheese toward one edge of the plate. Lower the scoop to plate level before releasing the goat cheese.

Use an eyedropper to form perfect circles of balsamic reduction that spiral from the center of the plate toward the edge. Touch the tip of the eyedropper to the plate and squeeze slowly to keep the circles perfectly round and small.

ROASTED ARTICHOKE BOTTOMS *with* SHRIMP *and* HERBED MAYONNAISE

Packing a large flavor punch into a small amount of real estate is one of the benefits of the minimalist style. This combination teams the bitter-woody flavor of artichokes, intensified by roasting with an herb mayonnaise, and sweet poached shrimp.

Choose a large plate for this arrangement. The colors, from the deep brown artichoke leaves to the pale pinks and greens of the shrimp and sauce, draw the eye directly to the food. Floating that combination on a sea of white intensifies the effect. Additional sauce—here streaked, but pooling is an option—finishes off the plate.

Using a paring knife, trim the bottom of a roasted artichoke heart flat so it sits securely on the plate.

Spoon herbed mayonnaise into the artichoke bottom. Fill the bottom halfway so it will not spill onto the plate when the shrimp are added.

Thin the mayonnaise with a small amount of hot water to make it pourable. Using a spoon (as pictured) or a squeeze bottle, paint thin stripes of sauce in more or less parallel lines, off-center of the plate. Start with a small amount of sauce on the spoon; the lines of sauce will be easier to control. Stagger the beginning and end of each stripe to add visual interest.

KENT RATHBUN

Executive Chef/Proprietor
Abacus, Jasper's
Dallas, TX

Kent Rathbun is executive chef and proprietor of two of Dallas's most talked about restaurants, Abacus and Jasper's. At the early age of seventeen, he began as an apprentice at La Bonne Auberge, a five-star French restaurant located in Kansas City. Rathbun's career goals led him to the Landmark Restaurant in the Dallas Melrose Hotel, where he was able to make annual trips to visit restaurant owners in Bangkok, Thailand. Through extensive research and experimentation, Rathbun developed a spectacular style of contemporary global cuisine, drawing on Southwestern, Mediterranean, American, Cajun/Creole, and Pacific Rim influences. This eclectic and distinct style is reflected in the Abacus menu.

In 1997, Rathbun decided to follow his dream and establish his own world-class restaurant, Abacus. Since its opening in 1999, Abacus has received numerous accolades, including Mobil Four-Stars, AAA Four Diamonds, and Five Stars from the *Dallas Morning News.*

Four years later, in 2003, Rathbun opened a second restaurant, Jasper's. Its menu is focused on the best of America's regional cuisine, including steaks, chops, fish, rotisserie chicken, salads, pasta, and pizza. After being open just a few months, Jasper's was named one of *Esquire Magazine*'s "Top 20 Best New Restaurants in America," and continues to impress all who enter.

I have been cooking for thirty years, so my plates have had a lot of time to evolve: from a dusting of chopped parsley at the beginning to some extremely intricate plates ten to fifteen years ago, when I was dusting the edges of the plate with everything from beet powder to carrot powder. I was into it at the time, but now I see that sort of thing was a bit overdone.

When I opened Abacus about five years ago, I started to become more of a minimalist. I began looking at the components of a plate and making each of them as perfect as I could. If the elements of a dish were a piece of fish, a sauce, and a vegetable, I made sure each component was perfect looking and perfectly cooked.

At the same time, I was scaling down the size of my portions, largely because of my first visit to Thomas Keller's French Laundry in Yountville, California. It seems to me that the difference between a chef who takes a big portion and scales it down and the plates at French Laundry is that Chef Keller is not thinking about turning a big plate into a small plate; he's thinking about a small plate to begin with. In other words, when a portion consists of three or four bites, the rules of how to present that smaller portion change radically.

The dish that made me get it was a rack of rabbit I had at The French Laundry. Most chefs take the loin from the rabbit; Chef Keller takes a pair of shears and trims the loin into a four-bone "rack of rabbit," like a miniature rack of lamb. I thought that was the coolest thing in the world.

My plates have become more precise and to the point. Each of the plates at Abacus is going to be four or five bites—you might want to make a meal of three or four of these plates. If something is going to sit on a slice of eggplant, that means I'm cutting a 1½-inch round slice of eggplant, not using a whole slice. Even when working with a minimum of ingredients, I like the plates to have some height, dimension, color, and architectural style. Smaller doesn't have to mean less interesting.

THE ARCHITECT

No one has ever accused Americans of going at something halfheartedly. When chefs—led by Alfred Portale of New York City's Gotham Bar and Grill—began to "go vertical," stacking elements of a plate one atop the other, things quickly spiraled out of control. Teetering constructs of precariously perched poultry may have looked impressive, but proved confounding to eat.

The architectural approach to plating has not been, and probably never will be, abandoned completely. Rather, keeping pace with the general trend among restaurant chefs toward sleeker plates, there has been a movement away from towering pyramids and toward more simply presented food. Chefs have rethought the best way to deliver the impact of an architectural presentation that is, above all, dramatic *and* edible.

There are instances where the elements of a dish, presented vertically—and knocked down in the process of eating it—work beautifully. This chapter contains several good examples. A stack of seared, juicy quail, garlic mashed potatoes, and braised Swiss chard are better—to most people's way of thinking—enjoyed together, rather than separately. (Think of a Thanksgiving-day forkful of turkey, stuffing, and cranberry relish, all dipped in brown gravy.) A cobb salad is tossed together before eating it, whether presented "horizontally" or as a tower with the dressing drizzled around the base rather than over the ingredients.

It is easy to imagine almost any dish (except soup!) as reconstructed in a vertical manner. The simple Stir-Fry of Chicken and String Beans on page 33 is simply plated in three parts: a sturdy "foundation" of chicken, topped with a layer of string beans, followed by a crown of sliced scallions and chopped cashews. A pyramid of airy greens and thinly shaved fennel—a study in pale green and yellow—uses layering to showcase the elements of a simple salad in a most dramatic fashion (see page 29). The same principles can be applied to any salad, from a classic Caesar to the mozzarella, tomato, and basil that make up an *Insalata Caprese.* Even pasta can be twirled into a "turban" with a pair of tongs and a twist of the wrist, giving it height and adding interest (see pages 73–75).

The goal of architectural plating is not to construct the tallest possible edifice, but rather to highlight the contrasting elements of a dish through the method of plating. Elements are carefully added one after the other to create a visually distinct but harmonious look. The end result can be something rather studied and precise (like the Stacked Cobb Salad on page 41) or something less pronounced like the plates Suzanne Goin describes as "having fallen from the sky" (see page 127).

Most importantly, "building" should be done to enhance the way a dish is enjoyed. Cutting through the layers of a salad, like the Fennel, Arugula and Frisee Salad with Toasted Hazelnut Dressing on page 29, the diner ends up with a little of each ingredient on the fork, which is ideal. And although the effect of architectural plating is completely different from any other style, it should not differ from other styles by being difficult to eat.

PLATES PRESENTED

————

FENNEL, ARUGULA, *and* FRISÉE SALAD
with TOASTED HAZELNUT DRESSING

STIR FRY OF CHICKEN
and STRING BEANS

ROASTED QUAIL *with* CHARD
and POTATOES

STACKED COBB SALAD

CHEF PROFILE: SHARON HAGE

FENNEL, ARUGULA, *and* FRISÉE SALAD *with* TOASTED HAZELNUT DRESSING

Plating salads of all types displays the advantages of the architectural style best. Here, the different textures, colors, and shapes of a fennel, friseé, and arugula salad create an airy, textured tower that is offset by swirls of golden hazelnut vinaigrette. It is also possible to create a striking look by tossing the salad ingredients together with the dressing, but keeping the elements separate emphasizes the qualities of each.

Part of the appeal of this plate is that the colors are all in the yellow-green family, from the pale ivory-green of the fennel through the mid-range tones of the friseé and on to the dark green of the baby arugula. Going a different route, one could choose completely different ingredients and colors for each layer. Just remember: Choose elements that differ in appearance, texture, and color, perhaps a base of hand-torn radicchio, a center layer of cross-cut endive, and a topper of celery leaves.

Cut off any stalks from the fennel. Cut the bulb in half through the core and pull off any thick outer layers. Thinly slice the halved fennel bulbs with cores intact. (A mandoline or other slicing tool works best for this.) Soak the fennel slices in ice water for 20 to 30 minutes so they curl. Pat the fennel slices dry before using.

Make a base layer of fennel, keeping the edge of the well of the plate clear for adding the dressing later. Gently arrange trimmed frisée over the fennel, keeping the layers distinct and the frisée loose.

Crown the salad with a few leaves of arugula, arranged as shown, or laid loosely over the frisée.

STIR-FRY *of* CHICKEN *and* STRING BEANS

Part of composing plates in an architectural style is to rethink the elements of a dish. Traditionally, stir-fried dishes are simply spooned onto a platter; the appeal comes from the precisely cut ingredients and a harmony of color and shape. In this approach, the elements are separated and spooned onto the plate into a rough pyramid. Not only does this presentation highlight the different ingredients, it affords an opportunity to season the components differently, adding more contrast from the eater's perspective. Adhere to the rule that—no matter which approach is taken—the presentation of a dish should not merely look good, but should enhance the experience as well.

Spoon stir-fried chicken onto a rough square on the plate, tamping it into an even layer. (If the plate is round, start with a square layer of chicken and vice versa.) Keep this bottom layer even and compact; it will support the rest of the pyramid.

Top the chicken with a smaller layer of string beans, mounding them slightly to form the next layer of the pyramid.

Center chopped cashews and sliced scallions over the string beans to complete the pyramid. Lower your hand to the level of the beans for more accurate placement.

ROASTED QUAIL *with* CHARD *and* POTATOES

This traditional combination of pan-seared quail paired with mashed potatoes and sautéed red Swiss chard is an example of using the architectural style for dramatic impact as well as for enhancing the way the dish is enjoyed. Cutting downward through the "stack" of ingredients combines the texture and flavor of the three elements. The base of mashed potatoes serves as a platform for the sautéed chard and lastly the quail. Thinly sliced red stems from the chard are cooked along with the quail and scattered on top to add another layer and visual interest.

Spoon mashed potatoes into a rough circle in the center of the plate, leaving enough room around the edges for adding the sauce later. (The circle of potatoes may be set off-center instead of directly over the center of the plate.) Smooth the top of the potatoes into an even layer. For a more formal presentation, pipe the potatoes onto the plate using a pastry bag and a plain or star tip.

Using tongs, pick up chard leaves one or two at a time from their ends and drape the chard over the top of the potatoes to serve as a bed for the quail. The top of the chard should be more or less flat, but a little unevenness will not hurt.

After setting the quail over the chard, spoon sauce around the edge of the plate, making irregular, not smooth, lines.

STACKED COBB SALAD

Rethinking the arrangement of ingredients is one of the hallmarks of the architectural style. Here, the ingredients of a traditional cobb salad are stacked one atop the other, purely for fun and looks. Just as the "spokes" of a traditional cobb salad last for a moment or two, until tossed together, this tower makes its statement, then tumbles into disarray as one starts to eat it. As with the Fennel, Arugula, and Frisée Salad on pages 28 to 31, choose layers of ingredients that complement each other in terms of flavor, color, and texture. (The ingredients should also be large and moist enough to hold their shape—coarsely chopped nuts, for example, won't.) Clearly defined layers are the key; picture this cobb salad if it had been plated after all ingredients were tossed together, then tamped into the mold.

Place a tomato slice over the center of a plate to form the base of the stack. If the tomato is very juicy, drain it on paper towels for a few minutes. Set the mold over the tomato slice. In this case an empty tomato can serves as a mold, but a length of clean, unused PVC pipe works equally well.

Spoon the first layer of the salad, in this case dressed chicken, into the mold. Gently tamp down the chicken to help the stack hold its shape after unmolding.

Continue adding layers, gently tamping down each, until the mold is filled.

Remove the mold from the salad, lifting it straight up to keep the stack intact.

SHARON HAGE

CHEF/PROPRIETOR

YORK STREET

DALLAS, TX

Sharon Hage graduated from the Culinary Institute of America in 1984 and moved to New York City shortly thereafter. In 1991, Sharon moved to Dallas, Texas, where she worked as regional chef for the Neiman Marcus Corporation and as the executive chef at the Hotel St. Germaine and Harvey Hotel DFW.

In May of 2001, Sharon opened York Street, nestled in the quiet of east Dallas, just blocks from the bustle of downtown. Inside the restored white wood frame house, guests are seated in a tranquil environment of soft grays, pewter chairs, and crisp white lines that all work together to showcase the colorful dishes that are Sharon's hallmark. Imaginative black-and-white photographs of people who have touched Ms. Hage's life hang on the walls, inviting discussions and creating a casual yet sophisticated atmosphere.

York Street seats only forty-two guests, allowing Sharon and her staff to offer special touches. Because of her devotion to the best seasonal items available, the menu changes almost daily with carefully thought-out wine pairings. Ms. Hage personally selected every piece of the assorted silverware and porcelain. A salad might be served on a finger-painted plate, an entré on white china or on a piece of square ovenware—all carefully chosen to showcase the food.

The stellar reviews for York Street have given Sharon a very high profile on the national culinary scene, including a James Beard Foundation nomination for "Best Chef: Southwest."

Photograph courtesy of John Ater.

I think plates should be made of components that taste great together and that food should look like what it is. Those two factors, plus making things easier for the guests to eat, are the elements I take into consideration when plating food.

At York Street, things that end up on the plate look pretty much like they did in the pan. Part of that is a result of the size of our restaurant. Even though it's in Dallas, the kitchen isn't Texas-size—we have a six-burner stove and that's about it. But to be honest, if tomorrow I walked into a huge kitchen with six stoves and thirty cooks, I don't know if I would do anything differently. Stylistically, I've come to know that this works for me. And guests are very responsive to the food here.

We reprint menus every day, and that's what makes this restaurant exciting for me. Sometimes we'll come up with a special that may not be the most appealing-looking combination, like a recent combination of roasted chicken, sauteéd cabbage, and heirloom applesauce. Eyes closed, it was perfect, but there was way too much beige for one plate. I wasn't about to throw something green on the plate just because it needed it, so I plated the whole thing on a chartreuse plate and it pulled the whole dish together. I keep an odd bunch of different colored plates on hand for just such an emergency.

It may sound unusual, but making sure the guests don't have to do battle with the food they've ordered affects the way plates look, too. Large steaks will be sliced, fish fillets served skin side up. It is both the appearance and ease of eating; we take the time to crisp up the skin of fish, and it's served skin side up to stay that way. On the flip side, guests can spot the skin and get rid of it right away if they're not into it. With the exception of things like veal chops and pork chops—where the bone is why some people order the dish—we take most of our meats off the bone. Short ribs and rabbit legs are braised on the bone for flavor and then taken off the bone. In the case of the rabbit, we give the leg bone a little twist just as it goes on the plate, and that gets rid of the bone and leaves the nuggets of meat behind. The short ribs are removed from the bone to yield a clean, rectangular shape that is seared just before serving to crisp it up. We'll serve that with whatever feels right for the season, *farro* with wild mushrooms in winter or corn relish in summer. The beef still has that braised, rustic flavor, but with a terrific color, and there are no bones to deal with at the table. Nobody has to wonder, "Where am I going to put this?"

There is always something like a big bowl of mussels or cockles to share as an appetizer. Instead of dumping the shells and sauce into the bowl, we use a pair of long tweezers to set them open side up and then pour the sauce over them. Again, it's a question of what's practical and what looks good: You have a chance to get rid of any shells that didn't open, and the sauce is poured evenly over the meat of the shellfish, but it also looks appealing. I used to serve a large aioli or garlic toast on the bottom of the bowl, but found a lot of them were coming back to the kitchen. So we started making spoon-size croutons and adding them to the broth at the last second. (That ease of eating thing again.)

Things change from course to course. Main courses are pretty much the protein item and the accompaniment. The sauce, the textures, and the flavor balance are already built in; I just need to arrange the elements to be pretty and easy to eat. But desserts are always more plated than other parts of the meal. They tend to need a little more "frou," as you're usually starting with something that is soft in texture all the way through. So the crispy, crunchy elements that add to the interest of the dessert also dress up the plate.

THE ARTIST

Cooking is, by definition, a blend of art and science. In order for short ribs to become tender, they must be cooked slowly in liquid to cover for a prolonged period of time. That's the science. Finishing the potful of ribs with an assortment of vegetables hand-cut into olive-shaped nuggets instead of serving the beef up with the original (and probably overcooked) pot vegetables is the art.

All plating styles involve artistic decisions. This chapter is dedicated to those chefs who handcraft elements of a plate, constructing shapes and flavors that are at once familiar and intriguing. At the core of this style of plating beats the heart of a naturalist—one who respects ingredients for what they are and what they add to a finished plate. But where a naturalist might serve a medley of roasted root vegetables—parsnip, turnip, potato, and carrot—as the perfect complement to lamb, an artist would turn those same root vegetables into a puree, keeping the pale roots separate from their cousin the carrot, then swirling them together on the plate.

Fashioning containers for specific foods is one method an artist can use to create visual interest and elevate an ingredient without losing its identity, its flavor, or its harmony with other elements of the plate. Think of roasting an onion to a golden caramel, and then removing the central layers to leave a sturdy but tender outer shell. Turn the inner layers into the base for a classical onion and cheese soufflé and return it to its onion shell. It is still an onion, but somehow more so. Slowly toasting grated Parmesan cheese to form a crispy basket for delicate greens (page 55) not only makes a distinctive plate, it adds to the flavor of the salad.

An artist can also show foods in a new way, or introduce a lighter note into a plate. The purely American meat and potatoes look of the seared pork medallion on page 58 is lightened up considerably with herbs sandwiched between two paper-thin sheets of potato and baked until crisp.

Some artists paint in oil; others with a palette of sauces that range from clear to creamy, sweet to savory, and are inspired by all the colors of nature. While the minimalist relies on a pencil-thin stripe of sauce to bring the plate together, the artist makes more conscious brush strokes (see Desserts, page 151, for sweet examples). These go beyond mere plate-painting, though, and become part of the fabric of a dish. The bright green of a pureed spring pea sauce, flavored with mint and left somewhat coarse in texture, not only adds color to the plate, but further complements the flavor of the lamb and rounds out the textures of the finished plate. And that is perhaps the most important aspect of this plating style—coaxing the most from ingredients without distorting their natural flavors or essence. Current plating styles are less about specific patterns, like the "spider web" on page 179 (though those still have their place), and more about free-form shapes, like dots and swirls. Today's looser, lighter sauces fit this trend nicely.

Whatever shape the components of a plate are given, or how the finished plate is arranged, the overall effect should be natural, never tortured.

PLATES PRESENTED

PARMESAN CRUSTED LAMB CHOPS *with* SWIRLED ROOT PUREE *and* PEA SAUCE

SEA SCALLOPS *with* GOLDEN PEPPER SAUCE *and* MESCLUN SALAD

SEARED PORK TENDERLOIN *with* CHIVE MASHED *and* BABY CARROTS

CHEF PROFILE: ANDREW CARMELLINI

PARMESAN CRUSTED LAMB CHOPS *with* SWIRLED ROOT PUREE *and* PEA SAUCE

This is a painterly approach to a plate, appropriate for the artistic school. The swirls of color created by blending two distinct root vegetable purees and the splash of bright green minted pea sauce set off the crispy golden lamb chops. Propping the chops up with their bones crossed dramatically adds dimension.

The elements that make up the plate are rustic, humble, but there is an elegance to the assembly that comes from the contrasting colors and shapes and their arrangement on the plate.

Spoon dollops of potato-parsnip puree and carrot puree side by side in the center of the plate. The dollops should be about 3 tablespoons each.

Swirl the two purees together using the back of the spoon (it is not necessary to swirl too deeply into the puree). Dip the spoon in water to clean it between swirls.

Make last minute adjustments before adding the lamb and sauce to the plate.

SEA SCALLOPS *with* GOLDEN PEPPER SAUCE *and* MESCLUN SALAD

Artistic can mean artisanal, as in this hand-shaped basket made of one ingredient—Parmesan cheese. The lacy texture and irregular edges of the basket make it the perfect container for a salad of miniature field greens. Sea scallops, pan seared to golden and set atop a silky smooth puree of yellow bell pepper, round out the plate.

The contrast between the simple colors and shapes of the scallops set atop a monochromatic sauce and the mixed shades and textures of the basket of greens makes this plate beautiful. The contrasting height between the two halves of the plate adds to the overall effect, too.

Sprinkle a circle of grated Parmesan cheese onto a preheated griddle or skillet. Make the circle more or less even, but don't completely cover the pan with the circle of cheese: The end result should be a lacy circle that is easy to bend when warm.

After cooking until golden, use a thin, flexible metal spatula to gently remove the Parmesan circle from the pan. Slide the spatula under the Parmesan circle to free it completely from the pan before lifting.

While the Parmesan circle is still hot, form a basket by centering the Parmesan crisp over a glass and pressing the edges of the crisp gently toward the sides of the glass. Leave the side fluted, rather than pressing the pleats against the side of the glass.

SEARED PORK TENDERLOIN *with* CHIVE MASHED *and* BABY CARROTS

A crowning unexpected touch can make a big difference in an already attractive plate. It is the simplicity of the chief elements of the plate—pork, carrots, and mashed potatoes—that makes the artistic touch of translucent slices of potato framing a simple geometric shape made of sliced chive even more striking.

Slice a peeled potato thinly on a mandoline or similar slicing tool. If you are able, you can slice the potato with a knife, as long the slice is thin enough to read through.

Sandwich herbs between two potato slices, pressing out the air and making sure the edges are even as you go. Keep the herbs centered and away from the edges of the potato slices so the starch in the potato will seal the slices together. (See page 194 for directions for cooking the potato "chips.")

After baking, anchor the herbed potato crisp in the mashed potatoes. For the most dramatic effect, sink as little of the potato crisp into the mashed potatoes as possible while keeping the crisp anchored.

ANDREW CARMELLINI

Chef
A Voce
New York, NY

Born and raised in Seven Hills, Ohio, Andrew learned about food from parents who searched out organic products, small growers and old-fashioned artisans long before such things were fashionable. They taught him to love simple, delicious food made well—the best house-made sausages in town, the most flavorful ice cream, the hand-crafted Amish cheeses and right-out-of-the-field produce at the farmers' market.

Andrew graduated from the Culinary Institute of America, and by age 20, he was at work on the line at San Domenico, the haute Italian restaurant on Central Park South in Manhattan. There he learned the basics of authentic fine Italian cooking. Then he went to the source: he traveled, studied and cooked in Italy, working on the line under Valentino Mercatile, the highly regarded chef of the Michelin two-star San Domenico in Emilio-Romagna.

Back in New York Andrew served as chef de partie at Lespinasse, in New York's St. Regis Hotel. There he returned to the discipline of haute French cuisine—but he also learned to take risks, to bring together flavors and culinary traditions from around the world with respect and with elegance. During his time there, Lespinasse earned a four-star review from the *New York Times*. Three years later, Andrew was sous chef at Le Cirque when that restaurant regained its fourth *New York Times* star. Andrew also lived for a time in France and England, where he spent time in a number of top restaurant kitchens.

In 1998, after two years at Le Cirque, Andrew was recruited for the top toque position at the new Café Boulud. In his six years at Café, Andrew won a James Beard Award for Rising Star Chef of the Year and was named to *Food & Wine* Magazine's 10 Best New Chefs roster. In *Gourmet* in 2002, Jonathan Gold wrote, "Andrew Carmellini's modernist riffs on traditional seasonal bistro cooking, laced with Greenmarket vegetable worship and leavened with an international list of rotating specialties, are the sorts of things you can eat every day." In 2004, Frank Bruni celebrated this "first-rate" chef's "comforting, seductive" and altogether "glorious food" in the *New York Times*. In his final month there, Andrew won the James Beard Foundation's Best Chef: New York City award.

At A Voce, Andrew's seasonal Italian cookery is exactly the sort of fare that food lovers want to eat every day. At once stylish and earthy, carefully crafted and intensely flavorful, his food is refined by uncompromising technique. Laid-back and delicious, Andrew's food is informed by the wide world and deeply placed.

For me, plating is more about the concept or origin of a dish and less about pieces on a plate. The inspiration for my plates comes from the flavor profiles of what I'm cooking, the ingredients that go into a dish. I tend to keep flavors of dishes traditional, whether I'm making an Italian pasta dish or a curry from India or Thailand. If the dish is something very ethnic, like a curry or a Japanese dish, I'll search out the right kind of plate. Dishes that are less identifiable with a particular culture go on stark white plates that really show off the components. In either case, the dish itself is an important part of the plating decision. I feel the same way about presentation that I do about cooking: Even though I make dishes from many cultures and traditions, I stick to pretty traditional plating. I never present Western-style dishes on Eastern plates or vice versa.

For example, when I was at Café Boulud there was no room in the dining room for a proper cheese board display, but I love serving cheese as part of a meal. So I gave my dad a sushi board that I picked up in a restaurant supply store and asked him to replicate it. He made several, in maple, and they look terrific. They are functional—you can cut right on them—and they show off the cheese nicely, but they also inject a little bit of fun.

I feel there is a little more room to play with cold plates than with hot. I like serious color contrasts: maybe clear glass plates for raw fish with streaks of colored and flavored oil for flavor and contrast. The simplest things are sometimes the hardest to do successfully. Our clients love a simple, green salad, and for years I changed the plate and the salad itself looking for the perfect way to serve one. I happened upon a deep, very round bowl and knew I had found the answer. Not only does the salad look beautiful, but guests can better toss the salad with the dressing and eat it more comfortably. It's good for a chef to sit in the customer's chair. That's how I decided to plate the salad in that way. As a chef, you spend time stacking ingredients, only to have customers tear down the stack and dig in. It's easier to toss a salad in a bowl, to evenly dress the greens. These things are meant to be eaten.

American cooking has matured in that way, I think, from molds and an overuse of vertical plating and extra garnishes to more simplicity. I am very much into presentation on a plate, but never by dabbing extra garnishes all over the plate; then you're just confusing the focus of the dish. Again, it all comes back to the ingredients, and letting them do the work.

CONTEMPORARY EUROPEAN STYLE

Just as Americans in the United States were waking up to real French cooking in the late '70s, nouvelle cuisine with its radical presentations and exotic ingredients steamrolled through France. Things in the French kitchen have never been the same. Influences from Japan, ingredients from around the world, and a generation of tradition-busting chefs left us with plates that no one at the time would have recognized as "French." At about the same time, Americans began to explore the varied cooking of Italy's many regions and learned there was a lot more to Italian cooking than red sauce and pepperoni. And on it went with the familiar or undiscovered cooking of the entire European continent, as we adjusted our lenses to bring an enormous array of dishes and ingredients into sharper focus.

The plates featured in this chapter are not so much about the continent of Europe (quite a large geographic swath to reduce to generalities) as about contemporary versions of classical presentations: appetizers that set the stage for main courses of a certain size that, even with the trend toward dinners made up of smaller courses, hold their ground. This is as it should be. Some things, lamb shanks, for instance, are meant to be enjoyed in all their undiminished, meaty glory. Currently, espresso cups filled with foaming, intensely flavored soups kick off many tasting menus. They are savored for an instant, but anyone who knows and loves good soup also knows that a bowlful doesn't get really good until you're halfway through it. These presentations are a tribute to that spirit of sitting and lingering over a plate, taking time to pick the last of the meat from a bone, and savor the last spoonful of sauce or leaf of lettuce.

Traditional plating of these favorites has given way from dowdy and predictable to colorful and creative. While these plates are "protein-centric"—that is, they revolve around a portion of meat, fish, or poultry—they feel and look modern and reflect the best in current kitchen methods and a timeless pairing of ingredients. The above-mentioned lamb shank, for example, can be served upright, with a lighter sauce that is strained to give it a satiny look and feel, then enriched with swirls of sauce in a contrasting color. The plate is finished by molding risotto to bring it into scale with the lamb shank. The look is new, modern, but the flavor is definitely old school. Even though the meat, fish, or poultry still occupies center stage, much of attention is on the co-stars—vegetables, sauces, rice, pasta, and other accompaniments—which are used to show off the protein element to its best by complementing its shape, color, and scale.

Classic dishes, like the Skate Grenobloise on page 72, are classics for a reason: giving rich, moist skate a crispy crust and then pairing it with the bite of caper and lemon is genius. Instead of chucking the idea altogether, you can update it with angel hair pasta, tossed with nuggets of vegetables and some of the skate sauce. Everything old is new again.

Today in general, sauces are lighter, looser than classical sauces or even the reduction sauces of the nouvelle cuisine era. This means working with a lighter color palette and knowing that the sauces will cover more of the plate. More than ever, the sauce (if any) chosen for the meat, fish, or poultry must work with the flavor and color of the accompaniments.

To distill the essence of contemporary European plating remember these guidelines: a harmony of color, shape, and scale.

PLATES PRESENTED

BRAISED LAMB SHANK
with SAFFRON-PEA RISOTTO

SKATE *and* ANGEL HAIR PASTA
with CAPER BUTTER

MUSSEL CHOWDER
with HERBED OLIVE OIL

PAN-FRIED HALIBUT
with OYSTER-FENNEL BROTH

CHEF PROFILE: JAMES LAIRD

BRAISED LAMB SHANK *with* SAFFRON-PEA RISOTTO

In traditional dining, meat, fish, or poultry takes center stage in a meal, both in its central position in a meal and in its prominence in the main course. This pairing of slowly braised lamb shank and colorful pea-studded risotto shows there is room for improvisation on the meat-and-potatoes theme. First, by standing the lamb shank on end, the plate is given height, drama, and distinction. The accompanying saffron-pea risotto is also given height and drama. Down on plate level, the strained sauce and swirls of contrasting garlic cream add finishing touches. There is a sharp contrast in color, but also in style. Moving from rustic to refined, the eye takes in the natural form of the lamb, the timbale of risotto, and finally the delicately drawn swirls in the sauce.

After standing the braised shank upright, unmold the risotto onto the plate alongside the shank. (Drain the shanks of cooking liquid before plating to make a neater presentation.) Lightly oiling the mold before filling with risotto will help the risotto slip out more easily.

Strain the cooking liquid over the lamb shank to moisten all sides. Let the sauce run onto the plate and pool around the shank and risotto.

Using a half-filled teaspoon, make dots of garlic cream in the lamb sauce. Use the tip of the spoon to swirl the garlic cream into the sauce in a random pattern. Start with just a few swirls; it is easy to add a swirl but impossible to remove one.

SKATE *and* ANGEL HAIR PASTA *with* CAPER BUTTER

Another classic of the European kitchen, Skate Grenobloise is paired here with angel hair pasta that is seasoned with the same pan sauce that is spooned over the skate. Wrapping the skate around the turban of angel hair pasta does two things: It reinforces the bond shared by the two elements of the dish and displays the unique wing-like shape and structure of the skate fillet to its fullest. The elegant simplicity that defines contemporary European style is evident here.

Firmly grasp the angel hair pasta with tongs. It is helpful if the tongs grab the strands at more or less halfway along their length. Hold the tongs parallel to the plate and touch the tongs to the plate.

Pull the tongs vertical to the plate and, using the tips of the tongs, twirl the pasta into a turban shape. To keep the shape intact, open the tongs as little as possible before removing them. The starch in the pasta will help the turban remain intact.

Transfer the cooked skate fillet from the pan to the plate with a metal spatula, curling it around the base of the pasta as you slide it from the spatula.

MUSSEL CHOWDER
with HERBED OLIVE OIL

Soups are an odd case when it comes to plating. More so than with other plates, they must have some built-in good looks. Given their fluid nature, there is little to be done once the soup is spooned into a bowl: maybe a drizzle of cream seasoned with a complementary flavor, a zigzag of extra virgin olive oil, or a sprinkling of a friendly herb. That is the case with this mussel and potato chowder with its saffron color and neatly cut ingredients. The finishing touch is equally simple and elegant: A mussel still in its shiny black shell is set in the center. Rather than having the mussel disappear into the soup, it is given a sturdy platform made by raking some of the vegetables into the center of the bowl. It is a small step to take, but one with a big payoff in looks.

Using two forks, rake the mussels and vegetables into the center of the bowl to create a platform for the mussel in its shell.

For clearer herb oil, strain the oil (or let it settle; see page 189) before using. Use a very fine sieve or a sieve lined with a double thickness of cheesecloth for this purpose.

Using a half-filled spoon, drip herb oil drop by drop over the soup, forming small circles that float on the surface. Keep the circles distinct.

PAN-FRIED HALIBUT *with* OYSTER-FENNEL BROTH

Along with warm salads and sleeker plates, seafood served in broth is one of the trends that are here to stay. Clear broths highlight rather than obscure the natural colors and shapes of seafood (and other ingredients). In this presentation, the sliced fennel and oysters float freely in the clear, mushroom-infused broth. The colors are subtle and pretty, and the look is sophisticated and clean. In a manner of speaking the broth becomes the new plate, framing a presentation in much the same way as china, with its various shapes, shades, and sizes.

Criss-cross cooked halibut fillets in a shallow bowl, setting them closer to one side of the edge of the bowl to leave room for the remaining elements.

Ladle oysters, broth, and vegetables into the bowl around the fish.

Use a small spoon, half-filled with oil, to gently spoon extra virgin olive oil onto the surface of the broth in individual small circles, letting them float on the surface.

JAMES LAIRD

CHEF/PROPRIETOR, RESTAURANT SERENADE
CHATHAM, NJ

At age thirty-five, chef James Laird's critical acclaim spans from his home state of New Jersey to the larger culinary world. *The New York Times* named him "one of the best classically trained chefs in New Jersey," *NJ Monthly* rates his restaurant among "the best of the best," and *The Record* describes his cuisine "as a soft and subtle love song." He has been nationally recognized as well. In 2000, as a tribute to his creativity and expertise, James became the first New Jersey chef awarded the prestigious Robert Mondavi Winery Culinary Award of Excellence.

Upon graduation from the Culinary Institute of America, James traveled to Europe to hone his skills under the tutelage of renowned chefs Georges Blanc and Alain Pic. During the early 1990s, he held positions at Lespinasse, The River Café, and Aureole, eventually moving on to New Jersey's esteemed Ryland Inn. During his tenure as sous-chef, the restaurant achieved an "Extraordinary" rating from *The New York Times,* the equivalent of four stars. It was in the kitchen of the Ryland Inn that James met his future wife and business partner, Nancy Sheridan, also a CIA graduate.

On October 31, 1996, James and Nancy opened Restaurant Serenade. Critics immediately awarded Restaurant Serenade the highest accolades. Calling it a "peerless dining experience," *Asbury Park Press* restaurant critic Andrea Clurfeld raved about the "blissful harmony" between chef and ingredients that results in food "at once sophisticated and simple."

James works hand-in-hand with local New Jersey farmers to source the freshest produce, meats, and cheeses for his dining guests. He lives in Morris County, New Jersey, with his wife, Nancy.

If I were to describe my style of plating, I would say it is a mix of naturalist and contemporary European. My plates are a sort of cleaned-up country cooking. When I opened Serenade eight years ago, the food, and therefore the plating, was not so complicated. At this point, we have a well-trained group that has been with me for a while. That gives me the freedom to be more creative, more experimental. We do strive to make the presentation artistic. If it's a brunoise, it's a nice brunoise, done with care. A good part of my cooking is based on vegetables. That means a lot of work in prep and proper cooking. That of course adds to the polished appearance of the finished plate.

There's another aspect of working with ingredients that's worth mentioning. Serenade is known for its wine list, so the dishes are very wine-friendly: not too many acidic notes or sour or overly smoky tastes. If we do a smoked dish or use a smoked ingredient, it is always lightly smoked. Decisions like this affect the ingredients, and the ingredients affect the finished plates.

My plates change, depending on the time of year, but they're always ingredient-driven. I cook with the seasons. It doesn't make any sense to develop dishes in December that feature asparagus and tomatoes. It works out well, because the colors of Serenade's plates will sort of mimic the colors of the outdoors: browns and oranges of squash and sweet potatoes in autumn, for example. It turns out that the colors of the season are the way people want to eat in that season—braised short ribs and roasted carrots in winter, for example. That very simple approach works for me. In summer, fresh local tomatoes and basil feel right, look right, and taste best.

ASIAN INFLUENCES

It appears that sushi is the pizza of the new millennium. The fact that no place, from the local supermarket to airports in landlocked cities, would be without some sort of "sushi bar" was unthinkable ten years ago. Sushi was borne on a wave of Japanese cooking that, in turn, followed the tremendous interest in authentic regional Chinese cooking which opened Americans' minds to a myriad of ingredients, flavors, techniques, and styles of plating and serving food.

This interest in all things Asian coincided with two other movements in the nation's restaurant kitchens: a move toward cleaner-looking plates and a renewed interest in the plate itself as a showcase for the food.

Asian-influenced dishes share some things in common with minimal-inspired platings. There is a certain amount of open space left on the plate and a dearth of finishing touches. But as you can see from the photographs in this chapter, there is a great emphasis placed on the shape and arrangement of ingredients. The seared tuna (page 95) is trimmed into a compact rectangle before searing, which yields neat, square slices: their pink centers contrast with the crispy-brown surface. The overlapping slices—the importance of shape again—are set perpendicular to an irregular streak of wasabi sauce which further points up the symmetry of the tuna slices. This interplay among shapes carries through into all dishes plated with a nod toward Japan and China. Watching a sushi chef working methodically, neatly, and calmly to trim the elements of a well-stocked sushi bar gives a clue to the importance of size and shape to this style of cooking.

The key elements of Asian-influenced plating in a Western setting are the simplicity of form and the importance of line. Both are beautifully illustrated by the simple pair of chives criss-crossed over the sliced seared tuna on page 95. Even the soba noodle salad (page 99), takes on a completely different appearance when wrapped in nori seaweed and shaped into a cone. Inside the glossy, black-green wrapper, the precisely cut strips of vegetables and cubes of tofu play off the serpentine, free-form buckwheat noodles.

The plate itself becomes important: Keeping things cooler and sparser, one could choose plain white plates, as was done in this chapter. Other chefs, like New York's Tadashi Ono (see page 102), consider the shape, size, color, and texture of a plate a vital part of the plating process. In either case, allow for some space on a plate to highlight the careful thought given to the shape and form of the ingredients. Sesame-crusted shrimp, with tails fanned and set upright on the plate (page 91), seem to stand guard over an asparagus salad on the opposite end of the plate. The asparagus salad, as simple as it is, is given another layer of visual interest by the Chinese technique of "roll-cutting." The spears of asparagus are rolled a quarter turn each time before they are sliced on the bias, giving them a more faceted look than they would have if simply cut diagonally into lengths. Like the precise cutting of the vegetables in the soba salad, a little knife skill goes a long way toward making a striking plate.

PLATES PRESENTED

————

SESAME-CRUSTED SHRIMP *and*
ROLL-CUT ASPARAGUS SALAD

SEARED TUNA *with* WASABI CREAM

SOBA-TOFU SALAD *in a* NORI CONE

CHEF PROFILE: TADASHI ONO

SESAME-CRUSTED SHRIMP *and* ROLL-CUT ASPARAGUS SALAD

A pairing of sesame-coated shrimp and a salad of bright green asparagus illustrates a few of the hallmarks of Asian-influenced plating. First, the amount of open space left on the plate draws the eye to the complementary elements of the plate. Second, the form of the elements is particularly important. The shrimp are stood on end to accentuate their dramatic crescent shape. At the other end of the plate, the asparagus are roll-cut (see page 91) before being tossed with the dressing. The contrast of the intriguing shape of the shrimp in and of themselves coupled with the pyramid of asparagus salad further reinforces the importance of shape in this school of plating.

Roll-cut the asparagus: After cutting off the asparagus tips, slice the spears on the diagonal, making an exaggerated diagonal cut.

Give the spears a quarter-turn before slicing them again on the diagonal. Each section of asparagus, instead of being sliced simply on the bias, will appear faceted.

Mound the asparagus on one end of the plate. Spoon the dressing slowly over the salad. As soon as you can see the dressing creeping toward the edge of the asparagus, stop spooning. The dressing will continue to seep and pool around the asparagus. Set the sesame-crusted shrimp, tail side up, on the opposite end of the plate.

SEARED TUNA *with* WASABI CREAM

Uncluttered plates, an emphasis on the shape of a plate's elements, and simple, modern design point to Asian sensibilities. Here, a tuna loin is carefully trimmed into a neat rectangle before searing. The results are nearly perfect square slices that, when overlapped, create a symmetrical geometric effect. A simple, free-form stripe of sauce points up the angles of the tuna; a free-form tangle of pousse-pieds (sea beans) adds another shape and additional interest to the plate. A white plate, just a few shades off the pale green color of the wasabi sauce, creates a cool, serene feel. Picture these same three elements—tuna, sauce, sea beans—plated on a deep brown or even black plate. What looks serene here would "pop" to create quite a different but equally interesting visual effect.

Cut the seared tuna at a 90-degree angle to make neat, square slices. Use one quick cutting motion to make even-edged slices.

Gently push the sliced tuna forward to create overlapping slices and expose the center of the slices.

Spoon a free-form wide stripe of wasabi sauce off-center on the plate. Keep both ends of the stripe from touching the rim of the plate.

Use a knife (or metal spatula) to transfer the slices over one end of the sauce stripe, arranging the tuna slices perpendicular to the stripe of sauce. If necessary, realign the tuna slices to make them perfectly even.

SOBA-TOFU SALAD IN A NORI CONE

Once again, the elements of this plate put on display the importance of shape in the Asian school of thinking. A salad of soba (buckwheat noodles), tofu, and vegetables is wrapped in a sheet of nori, the same type of seaweed used to make hand rolls in the sushi kitchen. By choosing to display the salad, itself an intriguing combination of diverse shapes, inside a geometric form, the cone, one is led to a take on the old real estate saw: When it comes to plating in the Asian/Western style, three things matter: shape, shape, and shape.

Picture the sheet of nori divided into four even squares. Pile the soba-tofu salad over one of the four squares. Keep the salad from spreading beyond the borders of the square.

Fold the opposite corner of the nori sheet over the salad. (*Very* lightly dampening the nori helps with rolling.)

Bring one adjacent corner of the nori sheet over the top of the salad.

Using both hands and grasping the roll gently, roll the nori sheet and soba salad into a semi-tight cone. Place the cone on the plate with its flap down to prevent it from unrolling. If necessary, tease a little of the salad out of the cone to spill onto the plate.

TADASHI ONO

Executive Chef, Matsuri
New York, NY

Tadashi Ono, born, raised, and trained in Tokyo, Japan, moved to Los Angeles in the 1980s, working first at the innovative French-Japanese fusion restaurant La Petite Chaya and then at the legendary L'Orangerie. Ono was best known as the executive chef of La Caravelle, one of the highest-rated French restaurants in America, and as executive chef and co-owner of Sono from 1999 through 2001.

Ono, having built his legend by combining French technique with subdued Japanese flavors, has used his appointment at Matsuri as a return to a more traditional Japanese menu, garnering some outstanding reviews from the city's hardest to please critics, from William Grimes at *The New York Times* to Jeffrey Steingarten at *Vogue* magazine.

For the last several years (at La Caravelle and Sono in Manhattan) I have been cooking as a Western chef and plating my food on white round plates. In those cases, presentation was more like painting on white canvas—pretty two-dimensional. Since I've returned to Japanese plating, I realize there are differences between Eastern and Western styles of presentation.

First, the plates are not always round, or white for that matter. I am using rustic plates with various shapes and colors. The plates may not be the most attractive on their own, but they make beautiful backgrounds for the food. In some cases, I pick a plate based on the food I'm serving. Sometimes I look at the plate and get inspired—it's almost like the shape, color, and finish of the plate is telling me what to cook.

Recently I went to a restaurant trade show and met a Japanese vendor who was featuring beautiful *bizan* plates. They are fired at very high heat, with no glaze. The wood ash becomes part of the finish, and the colors are neutral, from gray to dark brown and black. I immediately thought "sushi." The shape and color would benefit the colors of the sushi. A large plate with an oval shape suggests a whole fried fish to me.

Second, I notice that Japanese plating is more three-dimensional than Western plating. The very shape and cut of the ingredients are so important when I combine them. I was in Japan recently and noticed that even traditional restaurants are starting to take on some non-Japanese ingredients. Things like caviar, foie gras, and truffles are making their way onto the plates. Even though the ingredients may be new, the plating style is traditional. That is the way I feel about my food as well.

THE NATURALIST

On a warm spring night, a stone's throw from the Bay of Naples, I had the good fortune to share a meal with Tony May, owner of San Domenico restaurant in Manhattan. In a small, out-of-the-way seafood trattoria (that I never would have found on my own), Tony was talking about his life's passion—the food and cooking of Italy. During the conversation, Tony said something that sticks with me to this day: "In Italian cooking, you can tell what everything on your plate is." Italian food always seemed to me to be one of the least fussy ways to cook. But this comment of Tony's was, for me, a new way to look at the glorious cuisine of Italy.

The soul of Italian cooking lies in selecting the best fresh ingredients, playing around with them as little as possible, and building in flavors with judicious seasonings. In the case of the whole broiled fish I was dissecting with knife and fork at the time, that seasoning meant slices of lemon, sea salt, fresh thyme, and a drizzle of peppery olive oil when the fish reached the table. Indeed, if you were looking for a crash course in the naturalist style of plating, a trip to any part of Italy is all you would need.

At first, plating food that is as close as possible to its natural state may not seem like much of an art. But the naturalist style is, in some ways, more demanding than other styles. The goal of presenting food naturally is to celebrate the ingredients, not mask or camouflage the natural flavors, textures, or colors. Searching out seasonal, beautiful ingredients—even waiting for them to come into season—is an ongoing task.

Texture plays an important role in the foods and plating of the naturalist style. In the Butterflied Poussin with Rustic Bread and Tomato Salad shown on page 117, for example, the crusty, densely crumbed bread is torn by hand to give it as much surface area as possible to absorb the flavors of tomato, olive oil, onion, and basil. The effect is a salad that looks exactly like what it is—a peasant's way to use day-old bread. Think of "visual texture" as well when plating in this style. Imagine the appeal of a salad of red and yellow grape tomatoes, cut in half to expose their tiny seeds, tossed with whole celery leaves, roughly torn basil leaves, and red onion sliced so thin as to be almost transparent. This is a completely different look—and flavor—than the same salad made with finely chopped ingredients.

An abundance of herbs and greens, usually in large, free-form bunches, tucked under the plate components or wedged between them does more than reinforce the natural elements of a dish. The aromas from the herbs, borne by steam from the dish, engage a diner before the first bite is even taken.

Also, technique is everything to the naturalist. If you are flanking slices of a roasted shoulder of lamb with a gratin of asparagus, that lamb had better be perfect: seared to a rich brown on the outside, rosy pink and juicy in the center. One look at the tender spears of asparagus with their golden bread crumb and Parmesan cheese coating should speak volumes.

Most importantly, plating in the naturalist style is dependent on a sense of harmony— among ingredients, among flavors, and among the visual elements of the plate. (In a sense, this style of cooking and eating is the antithesis of the short-lived "fusion" cuisine fad, where chefs strove to combine ever-odder ingredients from far-reaching cuisines.) "If it grows together, it goes together," an axiom used by wine enthusiasts to describe the affinity between the wines and cuisine of a particular region, applies to these plates.

Most of the flavors associated with this kind of cooking are "built-in" flavors. The naturalist relies very little on sauces, other than simple pan sauces made by deglazing a roasting pan or sautés pan with stock and, perhaps, a little wine. The sweet taste of freshly caught bass, for example, is pointed up with a little lemon; free-range chickens need nothing more than a sage-and-thyme rub before hitting the sauté pan. To carry the above point a bit further, dishes composed in the naturalist style lend themselves more toward "dry heat" cooking methods: roasting, grilling, sautéing, and broiling. When you cook with these methods, foods tend to emerge at the end of cooking looking much the same as when they started.

The plates on the following pages are ingredient-driven and rely heavily on sound, basic cooking techniques. They are a springboard for you to start thinking about the combination of foods and flavors that best celebrate the season you're in now. Naturally.

PLATES PRESENTED

—————

SAUTEED BREAST OF CHICKEN
with WARM BIBB BEET SALAD

CREAMY POLENTA *with* WILD
MUSHROOMS *and* MUSHROOM JUS

BUTTERFLIED POUSSIN *with* RUSTIC
BREAD *and* TOMATO SALAD

SEARED SKIRT STEAK
with WILTED WATERCRESS

**CHEF PROFILES: TERRANCE BRENNAN
AND SUZANNE GOIN**

SAUTÉED BREAST *of* CHICKEN *with* WARM BIBB *and* BEET SALAD

Warm salads have become a part of the American canon of cooking. The most satisfying are those that unite the flavors of various ingredients while keeping the elements distinct. In this example, the pan juices from the chicken form the basis of the dressing in which sturdy Bibb lettuce leaves and roasted beets are tossed.

Remember to make ample dressing, which pools onto the plate and adds another design element. When plating warm salads such as this, keep at least one of the ingredients separate—in this case the chicken breast, sliced but still recognizable—to add diversity to the plate.

Remove the browned and fully cooked chicken breast from the pan. Leave behind the juices, which will serve as the base for the dressing.

After adding the remaining dressing ingredients to the pan juices (see page 191), toss the greens and vegetables— in this case beets and Bibb lettuce—in the pan juices to coat them and wilt the greens slightly.

Working with tongs, mound the warm salad on one side of the plate, leaving a crescent shape of open plate. Be sure to distribute the greens and vegetables evenly. Pour any dressing remaining in the pan over the salad and let it pool on the plate.

Slice the chicken breast diagonally for a more dramatic effect when fanning out the chicken around the base of the salad.

CREAMY POLENTA
with WILD MUSHROOMS
and MUSHROOM JUS

When looking at a naturalist's plate, one should always be able to identify its components easily. Here, golden-yellow polenta, pan-fried mushrooms, and the clear broth that results from cooking them all speak for themselves.

Spoons, or scoops, dipped in water would have lent the polenta a more polished look. The rough texture of the spooned polenta and mushrooms that retain their mushroom-y shape—signs of a naturalist at work—add up to a stunning and simple arrangement.

Use a large spoon to make rough egg-shaped portions of polenta, arranging the polenta spoke-like from the center of the plate. An oval ice cream scoop can be used instead of the spoon for a more formal presentation.

Scatter the mushrooms between the polenta, mounding them slightly.

Drizzle sauce over the center of the polenta, letting it flow into the bowl and pool underneath the mushrooms.

BUTTERFLIED POUSSIN

with RUSTIC BREAD *and* TOMATO SALAD

Roasted chicken, quail, or squab paired with Panzanella, a salad of bread, tomatoes, and olive oil, is a staple of Italian country cooking. Here, the bird is served butterflied—with backbone removed to help it lie flat on the plate. A rubbing with herbs flavors the meat and shines nicely through the crisp translucent skin of the roasted poussin. Panzanella, too, is given a twist: Instead of dicing day-old bread and tossing with the salad ingredients, a larger piece of bread, hand-torn from the loaf, is toasted, then moistened with the juices from the salad. The effect is even more rustic and is complemented by the butterflied poussin which flanks it.

Using a pair of kitchen shears, cut along one side of the backbone.

Cut along the second side of the backbone to remove it completely. (The backbone can also be removed by cutting along both sides with a heavy sharp knife.)

Separate the skin from the meat by wiggling a finger gently between them. Work carefully to avoid tearing the skin. Once they are separated, gently rub herb mixture under the skin.

Spoon juices from the tomato-onion salad over the toasted bread to soften it before topping with the tomato salad.

SEARED SKIRT STEAK
with WILTED WATERCRESS

The naturalist believes in keeping ingredients looking like what they are, not torturing them into unrecognizable shapes or forms. There is such a thing, however, as helping components of a dish look more like what they are. In this arrangement, the simple slicing of a steak makes it appear more steak-like. And watercress keeps its wonderful shape when tied into a bundle using a length of fresh chive. The end result is steak and a "bunch" of watercress which turns an even brighter green after wilting in the pan.

Tie the watercress into a neat bunch with a length of chive. Keep the bunch of watercress small—no more than you can hold in the ring made with your thumb and forefinger—or it will be difficult to handle and will not wilt evenly. Pick the longest, thickest chives from the bunch and immerse them in boiling water for 2 to 3 seconds to make them more flexible and less likely to break.

Trim the ends of the watercress bundle, making sure there is at least 1½ inches between the cut and the chive or the cress will slip out.

Wilt the watercress in a pan containing a thin layer of hot olive oil. Turn gently with tongs two or three times to wilt evenly. Season the cress and set in the center of the plate.

TERRANCE BRENNAN

Chef/Proprietor, Artisinal, Picholine
New York, NY

Terrance Brennan is the chef and proprietor of two highly acclaimed restaurants in New York City, Picholine and Artisinal. He began cooking at the age of thirteen and rose steadily to the ranks of America's most renowned and imaginative chefs. After serving as saucier at Le Cirque under Alain Sailhac, he worked in many of Europe's greatest kitchens, including Taillevent, Le Tour d'Argent, Au Quai des Ormes, Gualtiero Marchesi, and La Gavroche. Terrance's signature style took form while working under Chef Roger Vergé at Le Moulin de Mougins in the south of France. He returned to New York City and refined his art as chef at Annabelle's, the Hotel Westbury Polo restaurant, and Prix Fixe.

In 1993, Terrance opened his first restaurant, Picholine, which earned three stars from *The New York Times* and became widely known for its cheese course. Terrance extended his groundbreaking cheese service in 2001 with Artisinal. Paying the ultimate "homage to the fromage" in the spring of 2003, Terrance opened the Artisinal Cheese Center, a 10,000-square-foot facility dedicated to the selection, maturation, and distribution of the world's finest artisanal cheeses and home to five custom-designed cheese caves, the first of their kind in the United States.

When it comes to plating, I don't put a lot of emphasis on the "wow" effect. If you use sound technique, proper execution, and the right ingredients, you've got all the elements you need for a beautiful plate.

I think of the flavor combination first; not of the look or color of the finished dish. I am not going to sprinkle chopped yellow and red pepper around the rim of the plate just because the presentation "needs" a little color. Second, I think of the balance of the supporting ingredients and main ingredients.

A lot of what goes into my plating comes from what I want when I go out to eat. I order food from a menu based on the adjectives, by those things that are served alongside the main ingredient. If the menu says "tomato confit" and I get two slivers of tomato halfway across the plate, I'm not happy. I expect an intensely flavored confit made from great tomatoes to be an integral part of the plate, not an afterthought.

There are two sides of me; one who likes a clean presentation made up of precisely cut fish, a simple sauce, and a single accompaniment. The other side likes braised short ribs with vegetables, a gutsy daube of beef. I would say I am a mix of minimalist and contemporary European. But that doesn't mean these two things can't blend. You can add finesse to a plate of short ribs by wrapping the braised meat around a bone before plating it. As long as it's cooked properly and there aren't a lot of manipulations, the food should speak for itself. I don't like to make the food look like something other than what it is.

My plates are simpler now than they used to be. There aren't as many elements as there may have been in the past. Years ago, I probably thought about color too much, with flavor coming in second. As Asian cuisines become more prominent, I can see that style of plating becoming even more of an influence on my dishes. I appreciate that style of plating, say, a single item, like a fillet of red snapper beautifully trimmed and left whole, not sliced, afloat a pool of sauce. I look forward to finding expected and unexpected influences when it comes to plating. The art of cooking and plating should be an evolution.

SUZANNE GOIN

Chef/Owner

Lucques, AOC, The Hungry Cat (Co-Owner)

Los Angeles, CA

Suzanne Goin began her culinary career in 1984 when she interned in the pastry kitchen of the legendary restaurant Ma Maison as a high school senior. Leaving her native Los Angeles for Brown University late that year, she began her career in earnest at the award-winning Providence restaurant Al Forno and later cooked at Alice Waters's famed restaurant Chez Panisse in Berkeley. After two years, Suzanne moved to France to work, first at Didier Oudill's two-star restaurant Pain, Adour et Fantasie, then with Alain Passard at his three-starred Arpege in Paris, and finally at the fourth arrondissement's favored Patisserie Christian Pottier.

Upon returning to the United States, Suzanne was hired by Todd English as sous-chef of Olives in Boston, then as chef at Alloro, also in Boston. Suzanne returned to Los Angeles in 1995 to Mark Peel and Nancy Silverton's celebrated restaurant Campanile, first as sous-chef and finally as executive chef. In September 1998, Suzanne opened Lucques restaurant in West Hollywood with partner Caroline Styne. In July 1999 she was named one of *Food and Wine* magazine's "Best New Chefs of 1999." *Gourmet* magazine named Lucques one of the top six restaurants in Los Angeles in their October 2000 restaurant issue. *Bon Appétit* named Lucques on their list of favorite restaurants in September 2000, and *Saveur* magazine named it number eight on their list of 100 favorite things in January 2000. Suzanne and her business partner Caroline Styne opened their second restaurant, AOC, in December 2002, and Suzanne was nominated for a prestigious James Beard award in 2003.

I would call myself a naturalist. My goal is to show off the natural beauty of the food on the plate by using lots of local ingredients and letting them do the work. But it is safe to say that my plates have evolved over the years; they've become a little more complex. I do like plates to have a certain look, almost layered without being too tall. For example, I might plate a version of an antipasto salad made from interwoven layers of sliced persimmon, *jamon serrano,* crinkly market arugula, and shards of Parmesan, all dressed with a squeeze of orange, olive oil, almond oil, and toasted crushed almonds. I love the natural shape of the *jamon* and the beautiful mahogany colors of its meat. That's really all that plate needs to look wonderful. Whatever I'm plating, I bring three or four ingredients together and weave them into a sort of tapestry that looks like it fell from the sky rather than looking forced or manipulated.

The look of a plate is all built right in to the ingredients. Maybe I'll add a sprinkling of something at the end, but there is never anything put on a plate just because it looks good—the way the food "eats" definitely comes first.

DRAMATIC FLAIR

There are times when an understated or restrained approach to the art of plating simply will not suffice, times that call for an over-the-top showstopper—plates that are created for digging into and beholding. In other words, times to play with food. This can mean something as simple as lighting sparklers on top of a child's birthday cake or as sophisticated as fashioning bowls from tropical fruits to hold an exotic lamb curry or dusting a plate with spices in shades of rust and copper.

In a way, these dramatic presentations are easier to create than the elegant simplicity of a minimalist's plate or the restrained beauty of a naturalist's presentation. There are more elements and ingredients available to achieve textural, color, and height variations. And none of the standards that apply to some of the other schools of thought hold sway here. It is a much freer approach to the art of plating.

Even so, the food is meant to be eaten, not just stared at, a fact that should be taken into consideration no matter how festive a plate becomes. As in architectural presentation, what may be stunning to the person creating a plate can be downright annoying to the person eating it if that person requires a tool kit to disassemble the elements. Pick a theme and stick with it. In the case of Bird's Nest Brunch on page 144, the theme is obvious and lighthearted and the results are beautiful. Thin strips of scallion greens line the potato "nest," but also pair well with the crispy golden potatoes or the scrambled eggs. You should tie in elements of the dish whenever possible. Like the eggshell or the section of pineapple top on page 133, they need not be edible, but they should be functional in some way, as is the pineapple top, which serves as a way to anchor the skewers and give the whole plate a much more dramatic effect through height.

These dramatic plates tend to be colorful, and that is part of their appeal. The greens, violets, and yellows of the "nest egg" suggest spring; the vivid red, avocado, and muted shades of salmon and mauve in the seviche—all set off with a forest green palm frond— would be welcome at any Caribbean fiesta.

Exotic ingredients, or handling ingredients in an exotic manner, can be an important part of a dramatic presentation. Dusting a plate with cayenne pepper and ground cinnamon in neighboring shades of rust and red serves as a backdrop to a scattering of whole spices in a diverse range of colors, shapes, and sizes.

Above all, do not give up the spirit of the dish in search of effect. Plating two types of seviche—seafood marinated in lime juice, chiles, and herbs—together makes sense. They complement each other's color and flavor, and both play off the creamy-smooth guacamole that accompanies them. The drama here comes from plating them in a cocktail glass, side by side and over the guacamole. There is enough going on there that a poached, bright red crayfish (playing off the seafood theme) and an underliner of palm leaf (playing off the tropical theme) are all that's needed to take the plate to another level. Again, not everything needs to be edible, but it should serve a purpose: In this case the palm leaf frames and highlights the colors of the seviche and guacamole.

Yes, one could make a dramatic statement by choosing exotic or offbeat plates with wild colors, shapes, or dimensions instead of the white and clear glass examples shown here. But that is more about the plate and less about the presentation; what is truly interesting is investing plates with a sense of drama through the use of elements with contrasting color, texture, and height.

PLATES PRESENTED

———————

SEAFOOD-PINEAPPLE SKEWERS *with*
PEANUT *and* CHILE SAUCES

SEVICHE DUO *and* GUACAMOLE SUNDAE

LAMB *and* MANGO CURRY

BIRD'S NEST BRUNCH

CHEF PROFILE: EMILY LUCHETTI

SEAFOOD-PINEAPPLE SKEWERS *with* PEANUT *and* CHILE SAUCES

Incorporating some of the ingredients used to prepare a dish, albeit in different form, is one way to add impact to a plate. (See Lamb and Mango Curry, on page 141.) In the presentation of the chicken and pineapple skewers shown here, the top of the pineapple serves as a base for the skewers, giving the plate dramatic height and added interest in the natural form of the pineapple fronds. The yin-yang symbol, made from contrasting chile and peanut sauces, cross sections of star fruit, and a dusting of toasted coconuts and peanuts round out the plate. The key to success with dramatic plating is to keep the elements within a theme. Here the seasonings, elements, and ingredients are all, in one way or another, Southeast Asian.

After cutting off the top of the pineapple (with leaves), cut about one-third of the pineapple top at an angle, so the larger piece, with most of the leaves attached, can sit securely on the plate.

Start creating the "yin-yang" shape: Spoon peanut sauce onto the plate in an exaggerated comma shape to form the first half of the design. It is easiest to use a small spoon half filled with sauce to trace the outline of the comma, then fill in the center with the same small spoon.

Continue making the yin-yang design by using the chile sauce to trace the outline of the second comma and creating a circular shape with the two sauces.

Spoon the chile sauce into the outline to complete the design. If you like, add a dot of the opposite sauce to the widest part of each comma (see picture on page 133).

SEVICHE DUO *and* GUACAMOLE SUNDAE

Clear glass is the vessel of choice for this pairing of two different kinds of seviche served together with guacamole. From above or from the side, the effect is quite different. The lime slices, which create two separate areas for the seviches, are practical as they pair well with both the seviches and the guacamole. This dish is about color, fun, and freshness.

Fill a cocktail or martini glass about halfway with guacamole, tamping the top to make it fairly even.

Plant two slices of lime in the guacamole to divide the surface in half, creating two separate areas for the seviche.

Spoon one type of seviche onto the guacamole on each side of the lime divider.

LAMB *and* MANGO CURRY

The technique of dusting a plate has devolved from completely over the top (the entire plate and rim dusted with everything from pulverized mushrooms to chopped cilantro) to a more subtle use of color and texture. In the case of this presentation, the lamb and tropical fruit curry is served in a hollowed-out mango and is therefore self-contained, leaving plenty of room on the plate for expression. The rust and tan colors of the spices used to dust the well of the plate complement the color of the curry. The shapes and colors of the exotic spices—the same ones used to season the curry—are like subtly colored rock formations on a desert landscape.

Cover the plate sparsely with one type of ground spice (in this case, cayenne pepper). Use a very fine sieve and barely tap the side of the sieve to avoid over-coating the plate. It is best to practice on a piece of waxed or parchment paper to avoid clumping of the spices.

Repeat with the second spice (in this case, cinnamon).

Scatter whole spices randomly over the plate. Do this with your hand as close to the plate as possible so the spices don't roll or bounce when they hit the plate, blurring the sifted spices.

BIRD'S NEST BRUNCH

Pure fun: Pick a theme—in this case, spring brunch—and go with it. A nest of shoestring potatoes, lined with chive "grass" holds an eggshell filled with herbed scrambled eggs. Scattering edible flowers, like these violas, and pale green frisée over the open part of the plate rounds out the spring theme. A little topping of caviar—salmon is used here, but small black caviar such as beluga would work, too—add more "eggs" to the nest. The overall effect is a sense of lightness and freshness.

Snip an empty washed eggshell to create jagged edges. Leave at least half the shell intact to hold the finished scrambled eggs.

Carefully separate the two pieces of a frying basket and gently remove the shoestring potato nest. (See page 193 for complete directions for making the baskets.) Oiling the frying basket before filling with potatoes will make the potatoes easier to remove. If the potatoes do stick in places, gently pry them loose with the tip of a paring knife.

Curl several chives to line the nest and hold the eggshell steady. Wrapping the chives around your finger will curl them nicely.

After setting the eggshell securely over the chives, spoon scrambled eggs into the shell.

EMILY LUCHETTI

EXECUTIVE PASTRY CHEF

FARALLON RESTAURANT

SAN FRANCISCO, CA

In 1984 Emily joined the opening team of Stars Restaurant in San Francisco on the savory side of the kitchen. In 1987 she switched to her true passion, desserts. She was co-owner with Jeremiah Tower of StarBake, a retail bakery. Emily is the author of *Stars Desserts, Four Star Desserts, A Passion for Desserts,* and *A Passion for Ice Cream Desserts.* She contributed to the revised edition of *The Joy of Cooking* (Simon & Schuster 1997) and wrote the dessert recipes for *The Farallon Cookbook* (Chronicle Books 2000). She has been the executive pastry chef of Farallon Restaurant in San Francisco since its opening in 1997.

Emily's numerous accolades include the 2003 Silver Spoon Award from *Food Arts* magazine and the 2004 James Beard "Outstanding Pastry Chef" award.

When dessert plating started to really take off in the early 1990s, people got a little out of hand. They put tuiles all over plates, scattered mint leaves on everything, and topped tiny desserts with giant caramel spires, just as a garnish or frou-frou. I never went for that. In the middle of my career I went through a period of trying to do things because it was the trend. Once I gave that up I felt more relaxed; I could actually be more creative, and be true to my own style. I like to keep plates simple but elegant. Not simple like a slice of pie and ice cream, but in the sense that everything I put on a plate should look good but should also have a taste function. Components of a plate are not there just for visual impact. In the finished dish there should be a balance between its flavors and its appearance. I try to make my desserts both approachable and sophisticated.

When creating a dessert, some chefs envision first how it will look on the plate. They create from a finished idea. I do the opposite. When I visualize a dessert on the plate, it's an inside-out experience. I envision taking a bite of the dessert—how does it taste? How does it feel in the mouth? The plating comes last, after I have figured out the flavor elements.

You also have to make sure the desserts, both in taste and style, complement the restaurant. At Stars (San Francisco) where I worked for many years, things were more casual. At Farallon they are more refined.

I was in Tokyo recently and stayed at an absolutely gorgeous hotel, the Grand Hyatt in Roppongi Hills, and had a great meal. Dessert was a maple tart with ice cream. Very simple, but the presentation was unique. A whole, small tart was served on a little icing rack. Next to the tart was a little white "to go" container of ice cream. It was like having your own little tart and pint of ice cream for dessert. The Japanese do presentation so well, simple yet elegant and refined.

DESSERTS:
CLASSIC AND CONTEMPORARY

It may not seem that a tuna steak and an ice cream sundae have a lot in common and, in terms of flavor or appearance, they don't. But each presents opportunities and challenges when it comes time to present them. The previous chapters have dealt with matters of a savory nature and have defined broad categories and schools of thought to help describe the options available. This chapter, aside from dealing with that sweet part of the meal that remains some people's favorite, brings all those influences together in a single place.

On the savory side of the menu—appetizers, salads, soups, and main courses—the line between styles of plating is an easy one to blur, and few and far between are the chefs who would be willing to identify wholly with one camp or another. What is true for the savory side of the menu is true in spades for the sweet. Just as with all that comes before it, desserts in restaurants are plated to a great extent to reflect the restaurant in which they are being served. But, even more than with appetizers and main courses, the choice of how to present a dessert rests with the pastry chef who designs it.

Desserts can appear in a completely different light depending on how they are plated. White chocolate mousse (see page 175), in a glass streaked with chocolate and caramel sauces but otherwise left unadorned, becomes elegant and sleek. Rice pudding (see page 166), the uber-homey dessert, becomes chic when served in little egg-shaped dollops with a squiggle of raspberry sauce and fresh fruit to lighten the texture, color, and overall appearance of the plate. Either of those desserts fits into the minimalist style of plating. It is easy to imagine them plated differently: the white chocolate mousse in a chocolate tulip cup (see page 155) or a cup made of dark and white chocolate swirled together, with sauces drizzled onto the plate instead of lining the inside of a wine glass. And think how differently the rice pudding would appear in a glass streaked with the raspberry and mango sauces that adorn the napoleon on page 159.

Decorating the plate itself is one of the ways desserts distinguish themselves. Yes, painting with sauces and dusting with powdered spices is evident in main course platings, but it somehow feels especially at home on dessert presentations. As Wayne Harley Brachman explains (see page 182), be sure to choose sauces that complement the flavor, not just the appearance, of the dessert. In the case of the mini mocha tort on page 178, vanilla and chocolate sauces create a striking effect, but the simplicity of the flavors doesn't go to war with the complex taste of the tort.

Just as these plates borrow some of the techniques from previous chapters, there are ideas here that lend themselves to non-dessert items. For example, stenciling ground spices onto a plate in a geometric pattern, as is done with the cocoa and confectioners' sugar on page 162, might appeal to some more than the random sprinkling which accompanies the lamb curry in mango on page 140. In short, elements of all of the styles mentioned in previous chapters can be found in these desserts—often more than one in the same dessert.

WORKING
the PLATE

PLATES PRESENTED

———————

ALL-AMERICAN SUNDAE
in a CHOCOLATE BOWL

"SLOPPY NAPOLEON" *with* RASPBERRY
and MANGO SAUCES

WHITE CHOCOLATE-CHIP BROWNIE

RICE PUDDING QUENELLES
with FRESH FRUIT

PEAR POACHED *in* RED WINE
with RED WINE SYRUP

WHITE CHOCOLATE MOUSSE *with*
CARAMEL *and* CHOCOLATE SAUCES

MOCHA TORT CAUGHT *in a* SPIDER WEB

CHEF PROFILE: WAYNE HARLEY BRACHMAN

ALL-AMERICAN SUNDAE *in* CHOCOLATE BOWL

Borrowing a note or two from the artistic playbook turns an old-school ice cream sundae into a miniature work of art by handcrafting a bowl from melted chocolate. (Following the same procedure, with different size balloons, one could fashion containers for all sorts of dessert items from berries and mousses to sorbets and fruit salad.) In this presentation, the sundae itself is left relatively unadorned, making the bowl the focal point of the plate. Moving toward the dramatic school, one could trace squiggles of chocolate separately on parchment paper for decorating the whipped cream.

Begin creating a chocolate bowl: Holding the balloon by its tied end, roll the opposite end in melted chocolate. Work slowly to coat the balloon thickly and evenly with chocolate. You can determine the size of the bowl by how much of the rounded end of the balloon you coat.

Set the balloon coated side down on a parchment-lined baking sheet, pressing it gently to the paper to secure it in place.

Once the chocolate is very firm to the touch, pop the balloon and remove it from the bowl.

"SLOPPY NAPOLEON" with RASPBERRY and MANGO SAUCES

Going vertical—think seven-layer cake—is nothing new in desserts, but just as with savory salads and main courses, stacking or layering ingredients makes us think about them differently. Napoleon, the quintessential layered dessert, is usually a study in refinement, crisp edges and even layers. Here, the napoleon is softened quite a bit by preparing a looser pastry cream and using puffy, not flat, layers of pastry. With the addition of contrasting sauces—mango and raspberry—the effect is quite striking. Like the cobb salad on page 41, this is meant to implode as one starts to eat it, hence the name "Sloppy" Napoleon. The subtle differences in the color of the layers could be made more severe by dividing the pastry cream in half and tinting each half with one of the two sauces.

After securing the bottom layer of puff pastry to the bowl with a small amount of pastry cream, create alternating layers of pastry and cream, letting the cream flow from between the layers of pastry. Gently press each piece of pastry into the pastry cream to secure in place.

Spoon the raspberry sauce over the top layer of the pastry, letting it flow down the sides and pool in the bowl. Point the tip of the spoon in the direction you would like the sauce to flow.

Repeat with the mango sauce, allowing the two sauces to blend as they drip down the sides and pool in the bowl.

WHITE CHOCOLATE-CHIP BROWNIE

A little bit minimalist and a little bit dramatic, the geometric shapes dusted onto the plate with the help of cardboard stencils turn a plain white plate into a modernist fantasy. Here, circles were chosen to complement the shape of the plate and contrast with the square of the brownie. Take this basic principle—stenciling contrasting colors—anywhere you'd like to go: triangles, rounds, squares, or stripes, chosen to complement the shape of the plate and the dessert itself. Even a single element, like confectioners' sugar, can be stenciled onto a plate of contrasting color for a similar effect. This technique of stenciling plates is similar to painting or swirling sauces onto plates. The appeal of stenciling comes from crisp, clean lines between the two elements; painting with liquid sauces can produce clear lines, like the spider web on page 179, or a softer impression, like the sauces on the lamb shank plate on page 69.

WORKING
the PLATE

Gently tap cocoa powder through a sieve to almost completely cover the center of the plate and lightly cover the rim.

Secure cut-out cardboard shapes (here, circles are chosen) on a wooden skewer. It is easiest to slide the skewers through one of the corrugated ridges.

Rest the ends of the skewer on the rim of the plate to hold the cardboard shape in place. Use one or more skewers with one or more shapes to create different effects.

Barely tapping the sieve and keeping the sieve centered mainly over the cardboard cut-outs, coat the cut-outs well with confectioners' sugar to create a stencil effect. Lift the skewer gently, just barely off the plate and then off to the side, to prevent the confectioners' sugar on the cut-outs from sliding onto the plate.

RICE PUDDING QUENELLES *with* FRESH FRUIT

Think of serving rice pudding and you think bowls, cups, or, maybe, spooned into a parfait glass with layers of raspberry or caramel sauce to separate the layers. Here is a wonderful example of how presentation can transform our perception of a dessert through arrangement of the elements on a plate. By scooping the rice pudding into small, egg-shaped quenelles and setting them on an oversize white plate, they take on a sleek, modern look—far removed from the coffee shop scoop in an ice cream bowl. A zigzag of raspberry sauce and the natural color of fresh fruit bring the plate to life.

Using a spoon dipped in water, scoop up a mound of rice pudding. The mound should fit neatly on the spoon; overloading will make uneven quenelles.

With a second spoon dipped in water, smooth the rice pudding into an even oval shape.

Use a spoon dipped in water to coax the quenelle of pudding onto the plate. Lower the spoon to plate level exactly in the position you would like to place the quenelle before sliding it off the spoon; once on the plate they are difficult to move.

PEAR POACHED
in RED WINE *with*
RED WINE SYRUP

Presenting a whole pear poached in red wine harks back to the naturalist idea that some ingredients can be made to look "more" like themselves by handling them carefully. In this presentation, in which the pear is sauced only with a drizzling of the reduced cooking liquid, the naturalist meets contemporary European style. There is no mistaking this for anything except a pear, but the simple spiral cuts made through the pear give it a faceted and dressed-up appearance, as do the mint leaves and strips of lemon zest.

Using a melon baller and starting from the bottom of the pear, gently remove the core and pits from the pear. Work carefully, removing a small portion of the core and pits at a time to avoid removing too much of the pear along with them. (See page 195 for complete directions for preparing the pear.)

Starting about ¾ inch from the stem, make a spiral cut from the top to the base of the pear. Each cut should end up about one-quarter of the way around the pear from where it started. Make sure the tip of the knife penetrates no more than halfway through the pear.

Continue making similar cuts, about
1 inch apart, around the entire pear. The
more cuts you make, the less the pear
will hold its shape firmly, so be prepared
to steady the pear as you work.

Press the cut pear gently onto the plate
to secure it in place and separate the
slices. If necessary, separate the pear
slices gently with your fingers to enhance
the effect.

WHITE CHOCOLATE MOUSSE *with* CARAMEL *and* CHOCOLATE SAUCES

Here is a very simple way to go vertical with ingredients that don't lend themselves to stacking or layering. Soft-textured white chocolate mousse is piled into a tall glass—in this case an ordinary wine glass—that has first been streaked with contrasting sauces. Enough of the glass is left uncoated to see the mousse itself, creating an effect in which we seem to be peering at the mousse through a stained-glass window. This effect can be created in any shape of clear glass or bowl using two sauces of similar consistency.

Holding a wine or parfait glass horizontally, spoon a stripe of chocolate sauce along the side. This and subsequent stripes of sauce should start and end about 1 inch from the rim and bottom of glass. The sauces will be easier to handle and swirl more attractively if they are both at the same, lightly warmed, temperature.

WORKING
the PLATE

Give the glass a quarter-turn and spoon a stripe of caramel sauce into the glass; repeat with one more stripe of each sauce, giving the glass a quarter-turn before each.

Still holding the glass horizontally, slowly rotate the glass to blend the sauces. Stop just as the two sauces start to blend. Setting the glass upright at that point will finish the blending process and draw the sauces to the bottom of the glass.

MOCHA TORT CAUGHT
in a SPIDER WEB

Painterly plates have a special place in the world of desserts. According to Wayne Harley Brachman (see page 182), painting a plate randomly or precisely, as here, with two differently flavored sauces is more than eye candy. Each time the lucky person drags a piece of the dessert through the sauces, the effect and taste are somewhat different. This spider web design can be created easily with any two sauces of the same consistency, like the mango and raspberry sauces on page 159. As with all presentations, sweet or savory, location is everything. Spider webs like this, or any geometric patterns drawn with sauce, will have completely different looks depending on where they are drawn on the plate. Here, the entire well of the plate is covered and the web is centered. Alternatively, the web can be drawn off-center or onto only a part of the plate. Regardless of the location, the effect can be further altered by where the other elements are placed—centered over the web, as here, or set off to one side or another.

WORKING
the PLATE

Ladle crème Anglaise (see page 196) into the well of the plate, smoothing it into an even layer with the back of the ladle.

Using a squeeze bottle and working from the center of the plate toward the edge, make a spiral of chocolate crème Anglaise (see page 196). Squeeze lightly but steadily to create an even line. It is best to practice the spiral motion and the amount of pressure needed to create an even line on waxed or parchment paper before attempting one on a sauce-coated plate.

Starting at the center of the plate, pull the tip of a wooden skewer in a very straight line through the sauces to create a web effect. Make the spokes as close together or far apart as desired.

WAYNE HARLEY BRACHMAN

Chef/Owner, Swirl Ice Cream Parlor
New York, NY

Wayne Harley Brachman's inspiration is the flavor, fun, and nostalgia of American desserts: Everything he serves is innovative and absolutely yummy! *Time Out, New York* ranks him among the ten best in the city. His bold and hearty breads receive rave reviews. In 1998 he was voted one of the "Top Ten Pastry Chefs In America" by *Chocolatier* and *Pastry Art & Design* magazines. In 2000 he was the first American pastry chef invited to the Salon Chocolat in Paris.

Brachman, known for his quirky sense of humor, is now a popular figure on television. He was the co-host of Food Network's highly successful "Melting Pot" for four years and was regularly featured on "Sweet Dreams." Brachman contributes articles to magazines such as *Food Arts, Time Out, New York, Chocolatier,* and *Pastry Art & Design* and has been featured in periodicals including *Food & Wine, Gourmet, The New York Times,* and *The Los Angeles Times.* He is also the author of *American Desserts, Retro Desserts, Cakes & Cowpokes* and *see Dad Cook.*

Completely self-taught, Brachman was the pastry chef at New York's Odeon and then Arizona 206. From 1991 to 2000, he joined forces with Bobby Flay at Mesa Grill and Bolo. He lives in New York City with his wife and two daughters.

In the late '80s, when I was the pastry chef at Arizona 206, I first started thinking that there must be more I could do with plated desserts. In that era, it was a slice of cake on the plate. We concentrated on making the cake as beautiful as possible, but there was no real design on the plate, except maybe sauce painting in a couple of patterns that were pretty standardized—heart-shaped swirls, spider webs, and so on.

I began toying with ideas. When I moved to Mesa Grill, Bobby Flay started dressing all my desserts with sauces, working mostly with color as inspiration. My sous-chef Jimmy Skinner came up with the idea to do a pattern of sauce underneath the dessert instead of on top. It was just a little squiggle of sauce, but as soon as I saw that, the light bulb went on, and that was the beginning of painting my plates with sauces.

There were two motivators behind every plate: the way the finished dessert looked and, more importantly, that the sauces complemented the dessert. I didn't want to use two different color sauces just because they looked good; they had to make sense. For example, pumpkin cheesecake looked terrific set on a plate painted with pumpkin sauce and black sesame sauce. And it tasted great, too. And because of the pattern, every time you dragged a piece of the dessert through the sauces, there was a slightly different flavor.

Architectural desserts stemmed from the idea that desserts should look like something other than desserts. I never understood the principle. You don't want a piece of liver that looks like a couch, so why should your chocolate cake look like a cuckoo clock? As with savory food, desserts should look like what they are.

The trend is now for very simple presentation. (A reaction, I think, to architectural plates gone overboard.) I have kept things pretty simple all along; always approaching a dessert from flavor first, then design. The more I see, the more plating options, in terms of ingredients and flavor, are open to me.

PAINTING THE PLATE
SAUCES AND TECHNIQUES FOR FINISHING PLATES

DRESSINGS

TOASTED HAZELNUT DRESSING

When used in a salad (see page 29), dress the greens lightly and use a little extra dressing to decorate the plate. This recipe calls for toasting extra hazelnuts to use as a garnish in the salad.

MAKES ABOUT 1 CUP

½ cup hazelnuts, preferably peeled

½ cup olive oil

2 tablespoons sherry vinegar or white wine vinegar

1 teaspoon Dijon mustard

Salt

Freshly ground black pepper

Preheat the oven to 350°F. Spread the hazelnuts out on a baking sheet. Bake, shaking the pan occasionally, until deep golden brown, about 16 minutes. If the hazelnuts are unpeeled, transfer them to a clean kitchen towel, and rub them around inside the towel to remove the skins.

Coarsely chop the hazelnuts (or whack them with the flat side of a large knife). Put 3 tablespoons of the hazelnuts into the work bowl of a food processor. Set aside the remaining hazelnuts to decorate the plates. Add the olive oil, vinegar, and mustard to the hazelnuts. Process until smooth. Season the dressing with salt and pepper to taste.

PLATING NOTE: The mustard and hazelnuts will help keep the dressing from separating, yielding a fairly smooth dressing. If the dressing does separate, use as is for one type of look or blend the dressing briefly to re-emulsify it for a smoother look.

SESAME SEED VINAIGRETTE

Vary this by using toasted white sesame seeds, black sesame seeds, unhulled sesame seeds, or a mixture of the three. If using this as a plate drizzle, save some of whichever seed(s) is/are used in the vinaigrette to sprinkle over the center-of-the-plate item.

MAKES 1 CUP

3 tablespoons rice wine or white wine vinegar

1 tablespoon tamari soy sauce

¼ cup toasted (Asian) sesame oil

½ cup peanut or vegetable oil

3 tablespoons white, black, or hulled sesame seeds

Whisk the vinegar and soy sauce together in a medium bowl. Pour in the sesame and peanut oils slowly, whisking vigorously. Whisk again and stir in the sesame seeds (whichever type or combination) just before serving.

To toast white or unhulled sesame seeds: Place in a small skillet over medium-low heat. Stir or toss constantly until lightly and evenly toasted, about 4 minutes. Remove from the pan immediately to prevent overtoasting.

BLOOD ORANGE VINAIGRETTE

Blood oranges, with their streaks of burgundy and shocking orange, are perfect for plate decorations. Making a vinaigrette from the magenta-colored juice is beautiful, too. If blood oranges are out of season, try ruby grapefruits or tangelos prepared in the same way.

MAKES ABOUT 1 CUP

2 large blood oranges

Freshly squeezed lemon juice, as needed

3 to 4 tablespoons mild olive oil

Salt

Freshly ground black pepper

12 chives, cut diagonally into 1-inch lengths

Cut the ends off the blood oranges. Stand each orange on one end and remove the peel and white pith with a paring knife. Working over a bowl, cut the orange segments from between the membranes, letting them drop into the bowl. When all the segments are removed, squeeze as much of the juice as possible from the membranes into the bowl. Drain the segments and set them aside for the finished plate. Reserve the juice.

Add enough lemon juice to the blood orange juice to measure $1/4$ cup. Pour the olive oil into the juice, whisking constantly. Season with salt and pepper to taste. Just before plating, whisk the dressing to smooth it out a little and stir in the chives.

PLATING NOTE: The segments bathed in vinaigrette make a wonderful compote-like accompaniment on their own, as they do with the goat cheese and balsamic reduction on page 15. If using the dressing and segments to dress a salad of some type, make sure to feature them prominently: Use half the dressing to lightly coat the salad and spoon the rest onto the plate. Scatter the segments over or around the salad.

CREAMY BLUE CHEESE DRESSING

MAKES ABOUT 1 CUP

$1/3$ cup prepared mayonnaise

$1/4$ cup finely crumbled blue cheese, plus more coarsely crumbled blue cheese for the plate

2 tablespoons sour cream

1 tablespoon white wine vinegar

Large pinch cayenne pepper

Salt

In the work bowl of a food processor, combine the mayonnaise, blue cheese, sour cream, vinegar, and cayenne pepper. Process until smooth. Taste and add salt if necessary. This makes a dressing of thick, spooning consistency. For a dressing with a thinner consistency, suitable for drizzling, add hot water a few drops at a time.

Spoon or drizzle dressing onto the plate and top with coarsely crumbled blue cheese.

PLATING NOTE: For a different look altogether, like the blue cheese vinaigrette that accompanies the Stacked Cobb Salad on page 41, use red wine vinegar for better contrast and omit the cheese in the dressing. Spoon the vinaigrette onto the plate, and simply crumble the blue cheese over the vinaigrette on the plate.

YELLOW BELL PEPPER PUREE

This can be made with red bell peppers as well. Straining the sauce yields a silky texture. For added richness, whisk in 2 tablespoons of heavy cream or room temperature butter after warming the puree.

MAKES ABOUT 1$1/4$ CUPS

2 large, firm yellow bell peppers

2 tablespoons butter or olive oil

$1/4$ cup water

Salt

Freshly ground black pepper

Cut the peppers in half through the stem. Pull out the cores and seeds. Cut out the white ribs and tap out any seeds. Peel the peppers with a vegetable peeler and cut them into 1-inch pieces.

In a small saucepan, combine the peppers, butter, and water. Bring to a simmer, cover the pan, and cook over low heat until the peppers are very tender, about 25 minutes. Cool to tepid.

In a blender, puree the peppers until very smooth. Strain the puree through a very fine sieve, pushing it through with a ladle or the back of a spoon. Season to taste with salt and pepper. If you'd like to serve the pepper puree warm, heat it gently in a small saucepan just before serving.

PARSLEY PESTO

MAKES ABOUT 1 CUP

1 cup (packed) fresh Italian parsley leaves, washed and dried

2 cloves garlic

1/3 cup chopped walnuts

2/3 cup olive oil

1/4 cup freshly grated Parmesan cheese (optional)

Salt

In the work bowl of a food processor, combine the parsley, garlic, and walnuts. Process until the walnuts are finely chopped. With the motor running, pour in the olive oil in a thin, steady stream. When the mixture is smooth, add the cheese, if using, and pulse once or twice just to incorporate. Season to taste with salt.

The pesto may be refrigerated for up to one day. Press a piece of plastic wrap directly to the surface of the pesto to prevent discoloration.

PLATING NOTE: This makes a pesto of medium consistency, like the one shown on page 11. For a thinner pesto, more suited to drizzling or painting, slowly add more olive oil, with the food processor running, until the pesto reaches the desired consistency.

TARRAGON-CAPER MAYONNAISE

There are endless variations to this basic mayonnaise. Eliminate the capers, vary the herbs (summer savory, basil, and chives work well). If raw eggs are a concern, start with prepared mayonnaise and add mustard, capers, and tarragon, chopping them into the mayonnaise in a food processor.

MAKES ABOUT 3/4 CUP

3 large egg yolks

1 teaspoon prepared Dijon mustard

1 tablespoon freshly squeezed lemon juice

1/2 teaspoon salt

Large pinch cayenne pepper

1/2 cup olive oil

3 tablespoons capers, drained

1/4 cup fresh tarragon leaves

In the work bowl of a food processor, combine the egg yolks, mustard, lemon juice, salt, and cayenne pepper. Process until smooth. With the motor running, pour the oil into the yolk mixture a drop at a time until half the oil is added, and then in a very thin steady stream until all the oil is incorporated. Add the capers and tarragon and process until finely chopped. Scrape the mayonnaise into a storage container and store for up to three days.

PLATING NOTE: This recipe yields a fairly stiff mayonnaise, like that which is spooned into the artichoke hearts on page 19. To make a thinner mayonnaise for drizzling onto plates, simply thin out the mayonnaise with a small amount of hot water.

GREEN PEA SAUCE

MAKES 1¾ CUPS OF A COARSE PUREE
OR 1 CUP OF A SMOOTH, THINNER SAUCE

2 tablespoons butter

One 10-ounce package frozen baby peas, defrosted

2 tablespoons chopped fresh tarragon or mint

1 to 2 teaspoons freshly squeezed lemon juice

½ teaspoon salt

¼ teaspoon freshly ground black pepper

⅓ cup light cream, or more for a thinner sauce

Heat the butter in a 2-quart saucepan over medium heat. Add the peas, tarragon, lemon juice, salt, and pepper. Stir to coat the peas with butter. Cover the pan and cook until the peas are bright green and softened slightly, about 4 minutes.

Scrape the peas and butter into the work bowl of a food processor. Process until the peas are coarsely chopped. With the motor running, pour the cream into the peas and process to a coarse puree.

PLATING NOTE: Leave the mixture as is for a coarse-textured, thicker sauce, like the one that complements the lamb chops on page 50. For a thinner, smoother sauce, suitable for drizzling or painting, add 1 to 2 tablespoons more light cream and pass the puree through a fine sieve. The sauce will yield 1 cup after sieving.

MUSHROOM JUS

Making a clear, mushroom-infused broth for anything from polenta (see page 113) to pan-seared chicken and beef offers these advantages: terrific flavor and uniformly browned, delicious mushrooms that will further improve the appearance of your plate.

MAKES ABOUT 1 CUP

¾ pound exotic mushrooms, one type or assorted

1 cup boiling water

½ ounce dried mushrooms (about 1 cup)

1 tablespoon olive oil

Salt

Freshly ground black pepper

1 cup chicken stock

Trim any thick stems from the mushrooms. Cut them into large pieces (see Creamy Polenta with Wild Mushrooms and Mushroom Jus, page 113) to finish the plate. The pieces should be more or less of the same thickness so they cook evenly.

Pour the boiling water over the dried mushrooms in a heatproof bowl. Let stand until completely softened, about 20 minutes. Drain the mushrooms and reserve them for another use. Strain the soaking liquid through a sieve lined with a double thickness of cheesecloth or through a coffee filter.

Heat the olive oil in a skillet large enough to hold the mushrooms in a single layer over medium heat. Lay the mushroom pieces into the skillet and season with salt and pepper. Use a smaller skillet or plate to weight the mushrooms down. This will help them brown deeply and evenly. Cook until the underside is well browned, about 5 minutes. Flip the mushroom pieces and cook on the second side. Remove the mushrooms to a plate.

Pour the mushroom soaking liquid into the skillet and bring to a boil. Boil until reduced by half. Pour in the chicken stock, bring to a boil, and cook until the liquid is reduced to 1 cup. Taste and season with salt and pepper, if necessary.

CLEAR HERB OIL

These oils can be made with rosemary, tarragon, or basil. In any case, separate the leaves from the thick stems or stalks.

Plunge the leaves into boiling water for 5 seconds. Drain thoroughly, then pat as dry as possible with paper towels. Place the herbs in a blender jar and pour in enough olive oil to cover. Blend until the herbs are chopped very finely. Pour the herb oil into a bowl or highball glass and let stand for 1/2 hour or so, until the herbs settle to the bottom and the clear, green oil floats to the top. Carefully spoon or pour off the oil, leaving the sediment—which can be used to season soups, dressing, and other dishes—behind. Use within one to two days.

WASABI SAUCE

Wasabi is a natural thickener, and the same amount of wasabi powder needed to season the sauce thickens the sauce sufficiently to spoon onto a plate. This is the basic recipe; feel free to add interest with thinly sliced chives, chopped parsley, or diced roasted red pepper.

MAKES 1 CUP

- **2 tablespoons wasabi powder (see Note)**
- **1/2 teaspoon kosher salt**
- **1 cup half and half or light cream**
- **1 teaspoon freshly squeezed lemon juice**

Put the wasabi powder and salt in a small saucepan. Pour the light cream into the pan slowly, whisking constantly until the wasabi is dissolved.

Place the pan over low heat and whisk constantly until the sauce is simmering and thickened. Remove from the heat and whisk in the lemon juice. The sauce is best made just before using.

NOTE: Most "wasabi" powder sold is a combination of powdered horseradish, mustard, and other ingredients. 100% pure wasabi powder is rare, expensive, and will not thicken quite as well as the above-mentioned type.

PEANUT SAUCE

This is a mildly spicy sauce. Still, there are ways to lessen the heat in this sauce: Use a chile pepper or two less or tap out the seeds (where most of the heat is) before soaking them.

MAKES ABOUT 1 CUP

- **3/4 cup water**
- **2 tablespoons soy sauce**
- **2 slices peeled fresh ginger**
- **2 cloves garlic, smashed and peeled**
- **3 small dried chiles, such as arbol, stems removed**
- **4 ounces (about 1 cup) dry-roasted peanuts**

Bring the water, soy sauce, ginger, garlic, and dried chiles to a boil in a small saucepan. Turn off the heat and let stand until cool.

Put the peanuts in the work bowl of a food processor. Pour in the soy sauce mixture and spices. Process until very smooth.

PLATING NOTE: This will produce a thickish sauce for pooling (see page 133). For a thinner sauce more suitable to drizzling, simply thin the sauce with a small amount of hot water.

TOASTED CHILE PEPPER SAUCE

MAKES ABOUT 1 CUP

- 2 tablespoons vegetable oil
- 1 medium red onion, diced fine
- 2 cloves garlic, thinly sliced
- 6 small dried chiles, such as arbol, stems removed
- 1¼ cups chicken stock
- Salt

Heat the oil in a small saucepan over medium heat. Stir in the onion and garlic and cook, stirring often, until golden brown, about 8 minutes. Add the dried chiles and stir until they change color, about 1 minute.

Pour in the chicken stock and bring to a boil. Adjust the heat to simmering, cover the pan, and cook 5 minutes. Cool to room temperature.

Process everything in a food processor or blender until smooth. Using a small ladle or the back of a spoon, force the sauce through a fine sieve for a very smooth consistency. Add salt to taste.

FULL DISHES

LAMB SHANKS IN RICH RED WINE SAUCE

MAKES 4 SERVINGS

- 4 small lamb shanks (about 10 ounces each)
- Salt
- Freshly ground black pepper
- 2 sprigs fresh rosemary or 1 tablespoon dried
- 8 sprigs fresh thyme or 1½ teaspoons dried
- 2 bay leaves
- ½ cup vegetable oil, or as needed
- 2 medium leeks

- 2 large yellow onions, peeled and coarsely chopped (about 2 cups)
- 2 medium carrots, peeled, trimmed, and sliced ½ inch thick
- ¾ pound mushrooms, cleaned and sliced ½ inch thick
- 10 cloves garlic, peeled and crushed
- 2 cups dry red wine
- 8 cups chicken stock, canned low-sodium chicken broth, or water, kept hot
- 1 cup canned crushed tomatoes

Season the lamb generously with salt and pepper. If you are using fresh herbs, tie the sprigs of rosemary and thyme and the bay leaves together securely with a short length of kitchen twine.

Heat half the oil over medium-high heat in a heavy casserole large enough to hold the shanks. When the oil is hot but not smoking, add the shanks and cook, turning often with a pair of long tongs so they color evenly, until the lamb is a rich brown on all sides, about 10 minutes. Remove the lamb to a brown paper bag or paper towels to drain.

While the lamb is browning, trim the root and dark green leaves from the leeks. Split the leeks lengthwise and chop them coarsely. Place the leek pieces in a large bowl of cool water and swish to remove the sand and grit from between the layers. Let settle a minute and remove the leek pieces with your hands or a wire skimmer to a colander to drain.

Pour off all but a thin layer of fat from the pan. Add the onions, carrots, mushrooms, garlic, and leeks to the casserole. Pour in a good splash of wine—enough to completely moisten the bottom of the casserole. Cook, scraping the bottom, to release the browned bits which are stuck to the bottom of the casserole. Continue cooking until the wine is evaporated and the vegetables are lightly browned, about 10 minutes.

Add the remaining wine to the casserole and heat to boiling. Return the lamb to the casserole and pour in enough of the hot stock to barely cover the lamb. Heat to boiling, then adjust the heat to simmering. Tuck the herb bundle into the center of the liquid. (If using dried herbs, stir them and the bay leaves into the liquid.) Place the cover of the casserole slightly ajar and cook the lamb, turning the pieces in the liquid occasionally, until the vegetables are very tender, about 45 minutes.

With a slotted spoon, remove the lamb pieces and herb bundle to a large bowl leaving the vegetables and cooking liquid behind in the casserole. Transfer the vegetables with a wire skimmer to a blender. Add the crushed tomatoes and blend at low speed until the mixture is very smooth. Stir the vegetable mixture back into the casserole. Season the cooking liquid with salt and pepper. Return the meat and herbs to the casserole. Cook until the lamb is tender and the sauce is lightly thickened, about 45 minutes. Season with salt and pepper if necessary, and remove the herb bundle and bay leaves with a pair of tongs. Strain the sauce through a very fine sieve before serving.

SAUTÉED BREAST OF CHICKEN WITH WARM BEET AND BIBB SALAD

The following recipe can serve as a model for warm salads made with all sorts of ingredients, including beef steaks, duck breasts, fish fillets, shrimp, and so on. Select greens, herbs, and vegetables to complement the main ingredient. Prepare the greens and herbs, place them in a bowl, and add vegetables, cooking them first, if necessary (such as the beets), or adding them raw as you would chunks of tomato, grated carrot, or sliced cucumber. Add broth to deglaze—remove the brown bits that stick to the bottom of the skillet—and make a dressing with any kind of vinegar or lemon juice. Whatever you choose, have the greens and vegetables ready to go before you start cooking the protein component of the salad. Pour the dressing hot

from the pan in order to wilt the greens slightly. That is what brings the flavors of warm salads like these together.

MAKES 2 SERVINGS

1 bunch each red and gold baby beets

1 large head Bibb lettuce

2 tablespoons chives cut diagonally into 1-inch lengths

2 boneless, skin-on chicken breasts, preferably with first wing bone attached (see page 110)

Salt

Freshly ground black pepper

6 tablespoons extra virgin olive oil

½ cup chicken stock

2 tablespoons red wine vinegar

Cut the tops and leaves (if any) off the beets and scrub the skins. Put the beets in a large pot of cold water and bring to a boil. Cook until the beets are tender when poked with a paring knife, 15 to 25 minutes, depending on the beets.

While the beets are cooking, prepare the lettuce: Pull off any wilted or yellow leaves. Separate the remaining leaves and cut out any thick white stems. Tear the leaves in large bite-size pieces. Wash and dry the lettuce, preferably in a salad spinner. Put the leaves in a large mixing bowl and add the chives.

Rinse the cooked beets under cold water until cool enough to handle. Slip or scrape off the skins and cut them into 4 wedges each. Add to the bowl with the lettuce.

Season the chicken generously with salt and pepper. Heat 2 tablespoons olive oil in a large skillet over medium-high heat. Lay the chicken skin side down into the skillet. Cook until the skin is golden brown and crispy, about 8 minutes. Flip and cook until the second side is browned and the chicken is cooked through, about 6 minutes. Remove the chicken to a plate.

Pour the chicken stock into the skillet and bring to a boil, scraping the bottom of the pan with a wooden spoon. Boil until reduced by about half. Remove the pan from the heat and whisk in the remaining 4 tablespoons of the olive oil and the vinegar. Pour the warm dressing over the salad ingredients and toss to coat. Season to taste with salt and pepper. Mound the salad on one side of each plate, allowing extra dressing to pool onto the open side of the plate.

Slice the chicken breast on the bias and fan the slices of chicken out over the dressing, slightly overlapping the salad.

PLATING NOTE: Be sure to reduce the stock only halfway to make plenty of a dressing that will dress the greens as well as sauce the main ingredient.

SKATE GRENOBLOISE

Like the Sautéed Breast of Chicken with Warm Beet and Bibb Salad on page 109, this is a master plan for numerous variations. Angel hair pasta (see page 73) is the perfect accompaniment for the thinnish, liquidy sauce. And it looks impressive if wound into a turban off to the side of a plate.

MAKES 4 SERVINGS

4 boneless, skinless skate fillets, more or less of even size (about 2 pounds)

Salt

Freshly ground black pepper

All-purpose flour

3 tablespoons (or as needed) canola oil

8 ounces angel hair pasta

¼ cup small (nonpareil) capers

3 tablespoons chopped fresh Italian parsley

½ cup dry white wine

2 tablespoon freshly squeezed lemon juice

6 tablespoons unsalted butter, cut into small pieces

Preheat the oven to 200°F. Bring a large pot of salted water to a boil.

Remove any membrane from the skate fillets by slipping a thin-bladed knife between the membrane and the fish. Pat the fillets as dry as possible with paper towels. Season both sides of the fillets with salt and pepper. Spread the flour out on a plate and dredge the skate in it until both sides are coated. Tap or shake off any excess flour. Let the coated skate stand on a cooling rack (so the flour coating doesn't get gummy) while continuing.

Heat 3 tablespoons oil in a large, heavy skillet over medium-high heat until a corner of one of the skate fillets gives off a lively sizzle when dipped in the oil. Lay as many pieces of skate into the oil as will fit without touching. Cook until the underside is golden brown and crispy, about 6 minutes. Flip and cook the second side in the same way. If necessary, pour a little more oil into the skillet and repeat with remaining skate fillets. Keep the skate warm on a baking sheet in the oven while finishing the sauce.

Stir the pasta into the boiling water. Cook until al dente, about 3 minutes.

Meanwhile, pour off the oil from the pan. Add the capers and parsley and cook until sizzling. Pour in the wine and boil, scraping up the brown bits from the pan, until reduced by half. Pour in the lemon juice, remove the pan from the heat, and whisk in the butter until smooth. Pour off half the sauce into a small bowl.

Drain the pasta thoroughly. Toss the cooked pasta with the remaining sauce and add to the plates, twirling each portion into a neat turban shape. Plate one skate fillet on each of four heated plates, wrapping the thick edge of the skate fillet around the base of the turban. Spoon a small amount of the reserved sauce over each portion of skate.

SIDES

MARBLED ROOT VEGETABLE PUREE

MAKES 6 SERVINGS

1 pound russet potatoes, peeled and cut into quarters

½ pound each turnips and parsnips, peeled and cut into 1-inch chunks

½ cup light cream or half and half

4 tablespoons (½ stick) butter

2 large carrots, peeled and cut into 2-inch lengths

⅛ teaspoon grated nutmeg

Cook the potatoes, turnips, and parsnips in a pot of boiling salted water until tender. Drain, return to the pot, and let stand off the heat for a minute or two to dry a little. Add the cream and 2 tablespoons of the butter and mash. Keep hot.

While the potatoes are boiling, cook the carrots in a separate pot of boiling salted water until tender. Drain, dry, and mash with the remaining 2 tablespoons of butter and the nutmeg. Use a large serving spoon to drop the potato and carrot purees separately into the center of a plate. Swirl the two purees together.

PARMESAN BASKET

A well-seasoned griddle is the perfect place to make these. There is more surface area than a skillet and the lack of sides makes it easier to turn the Parmesan crisps over.

MAKES 4 BASKETS

1 cup very finely grated Parmesan cheese

Heat a griddle or heavy, nonstick pan over medium heat until a drop of water takes 3 seconds to evaporate. Working quickly, sprinkle ¼ cup of the cheese to make a 5-inch circle. (You will be able to make two baskets at a time if using a griddle or one at a time if using a skillet.)

Try to make the layer of cheese as even as possible, but it's fine if the cheese is a little uneven or if the griddle shows through in a few places. Cook until the underside is golden brown and the top is pale golden brown, about 4 minutes. Pay careful attention; once the cheese starts to brown, it will color very quickly. Over-browning the cheese will make bitter baskets. Slide a flexible metal spatula under the cheese circle to free it, then drape it over an overturned 4-inch bowl, pressing gently to form the cheese into a basket. Don't touch it until it has cooled completely. The baskets are very fragile, so move and work with them carefully. Repeat as necessary with the remaining cheese.

SHOESTRING POTATO BASKETS

Blanching the potatoes for a minute gives them a head start on cooking and makes it easier to curl the shoestring cut potatoes into the frying basket.

MAKES 2 BASKETS

1 Idaho or russet potato (8 ounces), peeled

Vegetable oil

Bring a large saucepan of water to a boil. Using a mandoline fitted with the julienne blade, cut the potato lengthwise into strips a scant ³⁄₈ inch on each side. Alternatively, cut the potatoes into scant ³⁄₈-inch slices, then stack two or three of the slices and cut them lengthwise into scant ³⁄₈-inch strips. Plunge the potato strips into the water. As soon as the water returns to a boil, about 1 minute, drain the potatoes and spread them out on a double thickness of paper towel. Pat dry and let cool completely.

Pour at least 4 inches of vegetable oil into a heavy pot. Heat over medium heat to 360°F.

While the oil is heating, dip both parts of a potato frying basket similar to the one on page 145 in the oil. Drain over the pot for a second, then use half the blanched potato strips to line the larger half of the basket. Spread the potatoes as evenly into the basket as possible. Set the smaller half of the basket over the potato strips to keep them in place during frying. Immerse the basket in the hot oil and fry until the potatoes are golden brown, 4 to 5 minutes. Repeat with the remaining potatoes. Adjust the heat under the pot as necessary to keep the temperature of the oil as steady as possible.

When done, free the potato nest from the basket, using the tip of a paring knife to gently free any stubborn bits.

HERBED POTATO "CHIPS"

Varying the size of the potato will give you larger or smaller chips. Smaller potatoes, around 8 ounces or so, yield 3-inch chips; larger potatoes, in the 10- to 12-ounce range, yield 4- to 4½-inch chips.

MAKES ABOUT 20 CHIPS

Vegetable oil

1 russet or Idaho potato (8 to 10 ounces), peeled

Small herb sprigs, such as chervil, cilantro, sage, or thyme, or chives cut into 1½-inch length

Preheat the oven to 350°F.

Rub a flat, sturdy baking sheet with vegetable oil to coat lightly. Slice the potato very thin—twelve slices should make a stack ½ inch high—using a mandoline or similar slicing tool. Keep the slices in a neat stack as you go. Arrange consecutive slices side by side on the oiled baking sheet. (Pairing consecutive slices keeps similar size slices together and makes neater chips.)

Center a small herb sprig or two lengths of chive over every other slice, making sure there is at least a ½-inch border around the edges of the slices. Cover the herbs with the neighboring potato slices, oiled side up. Match up the edges as closely as possible and press the two slices together to seal in the herbs and remove air pockets.

Bake until the underside and edges are lightly browned, around 6 minutes. Using a thin metal spatula, flip the slices and bake until the edges are golden brown and crisp, 3 to 4 minutes. Remove with the metal spatula.

DESSERTS

MANGO SAUCE

MAKES 1½ CUPS

1 cup mango juice

2 tablespoons sugar

1 tablespoon triple sec or other orange liqueur

1 tablespoon lemon juice

1 tablespoon cornstarch

2 tablespoons water

Heat the mango juice, sugar, triple sec, and lemon juice to simmering in a small saucepan.

Meanwhile, stir the cornstarch into the water in a small bowl until the cornstarch is dissolved. Stir the cornstarch mixture into the saucepan, stirring constantly until the sauce returns to the simmer and is thickened. Simmer 1 minute. Cool to room temperature before using.

RASPBERRY SAUCE

MAKES 1¼ CUPS

Two 9-ounce packages frozen raspberries (individually frozen, not in syrup), defrosted

2 to 3 tablespoons sugar

Lemon juice, as needed

Pour the raspberries and their liquid into a blender. Blend until smooth. Strain into a small heavy saucepan to remove the seeds. Stir the sugar to taste into the raspberry puree and heat to simmering. Stir until the sugar is dissolved. Cool to room temperature, then stir in the lemon juice to taste. The raspberry sauce will keep refrigerated for up to two weeks.

PEAR POACHED IN RED WINE

MAKES 4 SERVINGS

   1 bottle (750 ml) dry red wine

   1 cup sugar

   1 orange

   2 cinnamon sticks

   4 ripe but firm Comice or Bartlett pears

Pour the wine into a saucepan large enough to hold the pears snugly but comfortably. Add the sugar. Remove the zest (without any of the bitter white pith attached) from the orange with a vegetable peeler. Add to the pot along with the cinnamon sticks. Heat over low heat, stirring, just until the sugar is dissolved.

   Peel the pears. With an apple corer or the small end of a melon ball cutter, and working from the bottom of the pear, remove the core and seeds from the pear. Add the pears to the pot of wine as they are done.

   Pour in enough water to cover the pears. Bring to a boil. Adjust the heat so the liquid is boiling gently. Cook until the pears are tender when poked with a paring knife. Cool the pears to room temperature in the liquid.

   Remove the pears. Cut the pears, starting about $1/2$ inch from the stem and making spiral cuts toward the base of the pears (see page 172). The cuts should go all the way through the pear to the hollow center, but no deeper.

   Strain $1\frac{1}{2}$ cups of the pear poaching liquid into a small saucepan. Bring to a boil over high heat. Boil until the syrup is reduced to about $3/4$ cup and is thick enough to lightly coat a spoon. (Strain the remaining poaching liquid and refrigerate for up to two months for reuse.) Set the pear in the desired position on a serving plate. Press down gently on the top of the pear to fan out slices slightly. Pour some of the syrup slowly over the top of each pear, allowing the syrup to coat the pear and pool on the plate.

CARAMEL SAUCE

MAKES 1 CUP

   1 cup sugar

   $1/4$ cup water

   $1/2$ cup (or more) heavy cream

   1 tablespoon rum, optional

Heat the sugar and water to a boil, stirring constantly, in a small saucepan over medium heat. After the mixture comes to a boil, stop stirring and cook until the syrup turns a rich amber color, about 8 minutes; the timing will depend on the size and weight of your pan.

   Remove the pan from the heat and stir in $1/2$ cup of cream all at once. Continue stirring until smooth and shiny. Stir in the rum, if using. For a mellower sauce, stir in an additional tablespoon or two of cream. Cool to room temperature. The sauce will keep indefinitely if refrigerated.

PLATING NOTE: This and the Chocolate Sauce (recipe follows) will thicken as they cool. For plating, or to achieve a smooth swirl in a parfait glass as shown on page 175, it may be necessary to warm the sauces slightly. The simplest way to do that is in a heatproof bowl over simmering water. Also, for the best swirling effect the sauces should be of the same consistency.

CHOCOLATE SAUCE

MAKES ABOUT 1½ CUPS

   1 cup heavy cream

   $1/2$ cup sugar

   $1/4$ cup light corn syrup

   $1/4$ cup Dutch process cocoa

   1 tablespoon rum, optional

Combine all the ingredients except the rum in a small saucepan. Bring to a boil over medium heat, whisking constantly. Adjust the heat to simmering. Continue whisking and cook for 2 minutes. Remove from the heat, pour into a storage container, and stir in the rum, if using.

CRÈME ANGLAISE/
CHOCOLATE CRÈME ANGLAISE

MAKES 2 CUPS

2 cups half and half or light cream

½ cup sugar

¼ teaspoon salt

4 large egg yolks

Pure vanilla extract

Bring the half and half, sugar, and salt to a simmer in a heavy medium saucepan over low heat.

Beat the yolks in a small mixing bowl. Slowly ladle about ½ cup of the hot cream mixture into the yolks, beating constantly. Pour the yolk mixture into the saucepan and cook, stirring constantly, until thick enough to coat a metal spoon. As you cook and stir, pay attention to the bottom and corners of the pan; that is where the sauce will stick and scorch.

Pour the sauce through a fine strainer into a clean bowl. Stir in the vanilla. Press a piece of plastic wrap directly to the surface of the sauce (to prevent a skin from forming) and cool to room temperature. Chill thoroughly before serving. Crème Anglaise can be kept refrigerated up to four days.

For Chocolate Crème Anglaise: Coarsely chop 2 ounces bittersweet chocolate. Place in the bottom of the bowl before straining the Crème Anglaise. Let stand a minute, then stir until melted and incorporated.

INDEX

Italicized page references indicate
recipe pages.

A

A Voce (New York, New York), 62
AOC (Los Angeles, California), 126
Abacus (Dallas, Texas), 22
All-American Sundae in Chocolate
Bowl, 154–157
Angel Hair Pasta with Caper Butter,
Skate and, 72–75
Aquavit (New York, New York), 4
Architectural style, 25–26
Fennel, Arugula, and Frisée
Salad with Toasted
Hazelnut Dressing, 28–31
with minimum of ingredients,
23
Roasted Quail with Chard and
Potatoes, 36–39
Stacked Cobb Salad, 40–43
Stir-Fry of Chicken and String
Beans, 32–35
Artichoke Bottoms, Roasted, with
Shrimp and Herbed
Mayonnaise, 18–21
Artisinal (New York, New York),
124
Artist style, 47–48
Parmesan Crusted Lamb
Chops with Swirled Root
Puree and Pea Sauce,
50–53
Seared Pork Tenderloin with
Chive Mashed and Baby
Carrots, 58–61
Sea Scallops with Golden
Pepper Sauce and
Mesclun Salad, 54–57
Arugula, Fennel, and Frisée Salad
with Toasted Hazelnut
Dressing, 28–31
Asian-influenced style, 87–88
Seared Tuna with Wasabi
Cream, 94–97

Sesame-Crusted Shrimp and
Roll-Cut Asparagus Salad,
90–93
Soba-Tofu Salad in a Nori
Cone, 98–101
Asparagus, Roll-Cut, Salad,
Sesame-Crusted Shrimp and,
90–93

B

Balsamic Reduction, Herbed Goat
Cheese with Blood Oranges
and, 14–17
Basket(s):
Parmesan, 54–57, *193*
Shoestring Potato, 144–147,
193–194
Bibb and Beet Salad, Warm,
Sautéed Breast of Chicken
with, 108–111, *191–192*
Bird's Nest Brunch, 144–147
Bizan plates, 103
Blood Oranges, Herbed Goat
Cheese with Balsamic
Reduction and, 14–17
Blood Orange Vinaigrette, *186*
Blue Cheese Dressing, Creamy,
186
Bowl, Chocolate, All-American
Sundae in, 154–157
Brachman, Wayne Harley, 162, 178,
182–183
Braised Lamb Shank with Saffron-
Pea Risotto, 68–71
Breakfast of Champions (Kurt
Vonnegut), 7
Brennan, Terrance, 124–125
Brownie, White Chocolate-Chip,
162–165
Brunch, Bird's Nest, 144–147
Butter, Caper, Skate and Angel Hair
Pasta with, 72–75
Butterflied Poussin with Rustic
Bread and Tomato Salad,
116–119

C

Café Boulud (New York, New York),
62
Caper Butter, Skate and Angel Hair
Pasta with, 72–75
Caper-Tarragon Mayonnaise, 21, *187*
Caramel Sauce, 174–177, *195*
Carmellini, Andrew, 62–64
Carrots, Baby, Seared Pork
Tenderloin with Chive Mashed
and, 58–61
Chard, Roasted Quail with Potatoes
and, 36–39
Cheese boards, 63
Chicken:
Sautéed Breast of, with Warm
Bibb and Beet Salad,
108–111, *191–192*
Stir-Fry of String Beans and,
32–35
Chile Pepper, Toasted, Sauce,
132–135, *190*
Chive Mashed, Seared Pork
Tenderloin with Baby Carrots
and, 58–61
Chocolate:
Bowl, All-American Sundae in,
154–157
Brownie, White Chocolate-
Chip, 162–165
Crème Anglaise, 180–181, *196*
Mousse, White, 174–177
Sauce, 174–177, *195*
Chowder, Mussel, with Herbed
Olive Oil, 76–79
Clear Herb Oil, 79, *189*
Cobb Salad, Stacked, 40–43
Colors:
in architectural style, 28
in artist style, 48, 50, 54
in contemporary European
style, 66
contrasting, 63
in dramatic style, 130, 140
of foods and plates, 45–46

Colors *(cont.)*:
    in minimalist style, 5, 18
    seasonal, 85
Contemporary European style,
        65–66
    Braised Lamb Shank with
        Saffron-Pea Risotto, 68–71
    Mussel Chowder with Herbed
        Olive Oil, 76–79
    Pan-Fried Halibut with Oyster-
        Fennel Broth, 80–83
    Skate and Angel Hair Pasta
        with Caper Butter, 72–75
Creamy Blue Cheese Dressing, *186*
Creamy Polenta with Wild
        Mushrooms and Mushroom
        Jus, 112–115
Crème Anglaise/Chocolate Crème
        Anglaise, 180–181, *196*
Curry, Lamb and Mango, 140–143

D
Desserts, 151–152
    All-American Sundae in
        Chocolate Bowl, 154–157
    Caramel Sauce, 174–177, *195*
    Chocolate Sauce, 174–177, *195*
    Crème Anglaise/Chocolate
        Crème Anglaise, 180–181,
        196
    Mango Sauce, 158–161, *194*
    Mocha Tort Caught in a Spider
        Web, 178–181
    Pear Poached in Red Wine
        with Red Wine Syrup,
        170–173, *195*
    Raspberry Sauce, 158–161, 166,
        194
    Rice Pudding Quenelles with
        Fresh Fruit, 166–169
    "Sloppy Napoleon" with
        Raspberry and Mango
        Sauces, 158–161
    White Chocolate-Chip
        Brownie, 162–165
    White Chocolate Mousse with
        Caramel and Chocolate
        Sauces, 174–177
Dramatic style, 129–130
    Bird's Nest Brunch, 144–147
    Lamb and Mango Curry,
        140–143

Seafood-Pineapple Skewers
        with Peanut and Chile
        Sauces, 132–135
    Seviche Duo and Guacamole
        Sundae, 136–139
Dressing, Creamy Blue Cheese, *186*

E
Ease of eating, 45, 46, 63, 129
Ethnic foods, plates for, 63

F
Farallon Restaurant (San Francisco,
        California), 148
Fennel, Arugula, and Frisée Salad
        with Toasted Hazelnut
        Dressing, 28–31
Flavors, 124
    in architectural style, 32, 36
    in artist style, 47, 48
    in minimalist style, 7, 18
    in naturalist style, 106, 108
Flay, Bobby, 182
French Laundry (Yountville,
        California), 23

G
Goat Cheese, Herbed, with Blood
        Oranges and Balsamic
        Reduction, *14–17*
Goin, Suzanne, 126–127
Golden Pepper Sauce, Sea Scallops
        with Mesclun Salad and, 54–57
Green Pea Sauce, 50–53, *188*
Guacamole Sundae, Seviche Duo
        and, 136–139

H
Hage, Sharon, 44–46
Halibut, Pan-Fried, with Oyster-
        Fennel Broth, 80–83
Hazelnut, Toasted, Dressing, 28–31,
        185
Herbed Goat Cheese with Blood
        Oranges and Balsamic
        Reduction, 14–17
Herbed Mayonnaise, Roasted
        Artichoke Bottoms with
        Shrimp and, 18–21
Herbed Potato "Chips," 58–61,
        194
Herb Oil, Clear, 79, *189*

I
Italian cooking, 105

J
Japanese plating, 103, 149. *See also*
        Asian-influenced style
Jasper's (Dallas, Texas), 22
Jus, Mushroom, 112–115, *188*

K
Keller, Thomas, 23

L
Laird, James, 84–85
Lamb:
    Chops, Parmesan Crusted,
        50–53
    and Mango Curry, 140–143
    Shanks, Braised, 68–71
    Shanks, in Rich Red Wine
        Sauce, *190–191*
Layering, 25–26, 28, 40, 158
Luchetti, Emily, 148–149
Lucques (Los Angeles, California),
        126

M
Mango:
    and Lamb Curry, 140–143
    Sauce, 158–161, *194*
Marbled Root Vegetable Puree,
        50–53, *193*
Matsuri (New York, New York), 102
May, Tony, 105
Mayonnaise:
    Herbed, 18–21
    Tarragon-Caper, 21, *187*
Meats, boning, 45
Mesclun Salad, Sea Scallops with
        Golden Pepper Sauce and,
        54–57
Minimalist style, 7–8
    colors in, 5, 18
    finishing elements in, 8
    flavor in, 7, 18
    Herbed Goat Cheese with
        Blood Oranges and
        Balsamic Reduction, 14–17
    number of components in, 14
    Pan-Seared Red Snapper Fillet
        with Parsley Pesto and
        Radish Salad, 10–13

placement of components in, 7–8

repetition in, 10

Roasted Artichoke Bottoms with Shrimp and Herbed Mayonnaise, 18–21

shapes in, 5, 7–8, 10

Mocha Tort Caught in a Spider Web, 178–181

Mousse, White Chocolate, with Caramel and Chocolate Sauces, 174–177

Mushroom Jus, 112–115, *188*

Mussel Chowder with Herbed Olive Oil, 76–79

N

"Napoleon, Sloppy," with Raspberry and Mango Sauces, 158–161

Naturalist style, 105–106

Butterflied Poussin with Rustic Bread and Tomato Salad, 116–119

Creamy Polenta with Wild Mushrooms and Mushroom Jus, 112–115

Sautéed Breast of Chicken with Warm Bibb and Beet Salad, 108–111

Seared Skirt Steak with Wilted Watercress, 120–123

Nori Cone, Soba-Tofu Salad in, 98–101

O

Oil, Clear Herb, 79, *189*

Ono, Tadashi, 88, 102–103

Oyster-Fennel Broth, Pan-Fried Halibut with, 80–83

P

Painting with sauces, 48, 152, 178, 183

Pan-Fried Halibut with Oyster-Fennel Broth, 80–83

Pan-Seared Red Snapper Fillet with Parsley Pesto and Radish Salad, 10–13

Parmesan Basket, 54–57, *193*

Parmesan Crusted Lamb Chops with Swirled Root Puree and Pea Sauce, 50–53

Parsley Pesto, 10, 13, *187*

Pasta, Angel Hair, with Caper Butter, Skate and, 72–75

Peanut Sauce, 132–135, *189*

Pear Poached in Red Wine, 170–173, *195*

Peppers:

Chile, Toasted, Sauce, 132–135, *190*

Puree, Yellow Bell, *186–187*

Sauce, Golden Pepper, Sea Scallops with Mesclun Salad and, 54–57

Pesto, Parsley, 10, 13, *187*

Picholine (New York, New York), 124

Pineapple-Seafood Skewers with Peanut and Chile Sauces, 132–135

Plates:

in Asian-influenced style, 88, 103

colors of foods and, 45

for desserts, 149

for ethnic foods, 63

for salads, 63–64

shapes of food and, 5, 7–8

Polenta, Creamy, with Wild Mushrooms and Mushroom Jus, 112–115

Pork Tenderloin, Seared, with Chive Mashed and Baby Carrots, 58–61

Portale, Alfred, 25

Potato(es):

Baskets, Shoestring, 144–147, *193–194*

"Chips," Herbed, 58–61, *194*

Chive Mashed, 58–61

Roasted Quail with Chard and, 36–39

Poussin, Butterflied, with Rustic Bread and Tomato Salad, 116–119

Q

Quail, Roasted, with Chard and Potatoes, 36–39

Quenelles, Rice Pudding, with Fresh Fruit, 166–169

R

Radish Salad, 10–13

Raspberry Sauce, 158–161, 166, *194*

Rathbun, Kent, 22–23

Red Snapper Fillet, Pan-Seared, with Parsley Pesto and Radish Salad, 10–13

Red Wine:

Pear Poached in, 170–173, *195*

Sauce, Rich, Lamb Shanks in, *190–191*

Restaurant Serenade (Chatham, New Jersey), 84

Rice Pudding Quenelles with Fresh Fruit, 166–169

Riingo (New York, New York), 4

Risotto, Saffron-Pea, Braised Lamb Shank with, 68–71

Roasted Artichoke Bottoms with Shrimp and Herbed Mayonnaise, 18–21

Roasted Quail with Chard and Potatoes, 36–39

Roll-cutting, 88, 92–93

Root Vegetable Puree, Marbled, 50–53, *193*

S

Saffron-Pea Risotto, Braised Lamb Shank with, 68–71

Salad(s):

architectural layering of, 25–26, 28

Bibb and Beet, Warm, 108–111, *191–192*

bowls for, 63–64

Cobb, Stacked, 40–43

Fennel, Arugula, and Frisée, 28–31

Mesclun, 54–57

Radish, 10–13

Roll-Cut Asparagus, 90–93

Soba-Tofu, in a Nori Cone, 98–101

Tomato, 116–119

Samuelsson, Marcus, 4–5

Sauce(s):

Caramel, 174–177, *195*

Chile, 132–135

Chocolate, 174–177, *195*

in contemporary European style, 66

Sauce(s) *(cont.)*:
    for desserts, 152, 183
    Green Pea, 50–53, *188*
    Mango, 158–161, *194*
    in naturalist style, 106
    painting with, 48
    Peanut, 132–135, *189*
    Raspberry, 158–161, 166, *194*
    Rich Red Wine, Lamb Shanks
        in, *190–191*
    Toasted Chile Pepper, 132–135,
        190
    Wasabi, *189*
Sautéed Breast of Chicken with
    Warm Bibb and Beet Salad,
    108–111, *191–192*
Scallops, Sea, with Golden Pepper
    Sauce and Mesclun Salad,
    54–57
Seafood-Pineapple Skewers with
    Peanut and Chile Sauces,
    132–135
Seared Pork Tenderloin with Chive
    Mashed and Baby Carrots,
    58–61
Seared Skirt Steak with Wilted
    Watercress, 120–123
Seared Tuna with Wasabi Cream,
    94–97
Sea Scallops with Golden Pepper
    Sauce and Mesclun Salad,
    54–57
Sesame-Crusted Shrimp and Roll-
    Cut Asparagus Salad, 90–93
Sesame Seed Vinaigrette, *185*
Seviche Duo and Guacamole
    Sundae, 136–139
Shapes:
    in artist style, 47, 50, 54
    in Asian-influenced style,
        87–88, 90, 94, 98
    in contemporary European
        style, 66
    in dramatic style, 140

    in minimalist style, 5, 7–8, 10
    in naturalist style, 120
    natural vs. contorted, 48
    stenciled, 162, 164–165
Shoestring Potato Baskets, 144–147,
    193–194
Shrimp:
    and Herbed Mayonnaise,
        Roasted Artichoke
        Bottoms with, 18–21
    Roasted Artichoke Bottoms
        with Herbed Mayonnaise
        and, 18–21
    Sesame-Crusted, and Roll-
        Cut Asparagus Salad,
        90–93
Skate and Angel Hair Pasta with
    Caper Butter, 72–75
Skate Grenobloise, *192*
Skinner, Jimmy, 182
Skirt Steak, Seared, with Wilted
    Watercress, 120–123
"Sloppy Napoleon" with Raspberry
    and Mango Sauces, 158–161
Soba-Tofu Salad in a Nori Cone,
    98–101
Space:
    in Asian-influenced style, 87,
        88, 90
    positive and negative, 5
Spider Web, Mocha Tort Caught in,
    178–181
Stacked Cobb Salad, 40–43
Stenciling shapes, 162, 164–165
Stir-Fry of Chicken and String
    Beans, 32–35
Sundae:
    All-American, in Chocolate
        Bowl, 154–157
    Guacamole, Seviche Duo and,
        136–139
Sushi, 87
Swirl Ice Cream Parlor (New York,
    New York), 182

T
Tarragon-Caper Mayonnaise, 21, *187*
Textures:
    in architectural style, 28, 36
    in artist style, 48, 54
    in dramatic style, 140
    in naturalist style, 105–106
Toasted Chile Pepper Sauce,
    132–135, *190*
Toasted Hazelnut Dressing, 28–31,
    185
Tofu-Soba Salad in a Nori Cone,
    98–101
Tomato Salad, 116–119
Tort, Mocha, Caught in a Spider
    Web, 178–181
Tuna, Seared, with Wasabi Cream,
    94–97

V
Vinaigrette:
    Blood Orange, *186*
    Sesame Seed, *185*
Vonnegut, Kurt, 7

W
Wasabi:
    Cream, Seared Tuna with,
        94–97
    Sauce, *189*
Watercress, Wilted, Seared Skirt
    Steak with, 120–123
White Chocolate-Chip Brownie,
    162–165
White Chocolate Mousse with
    Caramel and Chocolate
    Sauces, 174–177

Y
Yellow Bell Pepper Puree, *186–187*
York Street (Dallas, Texas), 44